Golden Days Awheel

by

Albert Winstanley

OWL
BOOKS

First published June 1991
by
Owl Books
P.O. Box 60
Wigan WN1 2QB

ISBN 0 9514333 9 3

British Library Cataloguing in Publication Data

Winstanley, Albert, 1916 -
Golden Days Awheel
I. Title
796.640941

Designed and typeset by
Graphic Design Ltd., Wigan.

Printed and bound in Great Britain

Text typset via DTP 11.5 on 12.5pt News Serif,
using 800 d.p.i. laserprinter

Albert Winstanley was born in Bolton, Lancashire, in 1916.

He acquired his first touring cycle at the age of 16. In 1966, at the age of 50, he became eligible to join the 'Autumn Tints Cycling Comrades', a veteran cycling organisation founded by the late Tom Hughes of Wigan, in 1924.

Formerly employed as an Aircraft Technical Clerk, he now enjoys his 'Senior Citizen' and 'Veteran Years', with his still active pen and camera, leisurely cycling to old and favourite haunts, as well as searching for new cycling delights.

My many cycling friends and companions, who have their own Golden Days Awheel taking them to the freedom found out-of-doors. Particularly to those, who, down the years, have shared with me the joys, delights and adventures, related in many of the chapters.

FOREWORD

The *Golden Days Awheel* enjoyed by Albert Winstanley have been sent rolling throughout the pages and chapters of this book, you are about to read. They are rolling down quiet country lanes, through lovely valleys with brawling rivers, over remote moorlands, tracks, and mountain ways.

They are rolling from a cycle touring world of a past age, to today.

All the stories in this book have one thing in common — a sense of joy. Rain, snow, or sunshine make no difference. Albert's pleasure of riding his bicycle, and his delight with the countryside, and with nature in all her moods, shine from every page.

You are lucky to have the opportunity of joining him on his travels.

Luckier still are those of us who have shared journeys with him, for he is a delightful companion. His command of folklore and local history is astounding, and his knowledge of hidden haunts, and "out-of-the-way" eating places is unparalleled.

His sense of fun is unfailing and it will be your good fortune to read *Golden Days Awheel* by Albert Winstanley.

Sit back and enjoy the journey.

Johnny Helms

ACKNOWLEDGEMENTS

Though the writing and illustration of this book has been a source of pleasure, my cycle and my always enquiring pen and camera, have been introduced to many new friends as the chapters have taken shape.

Their help and assistance has been invaluable, and I should like to express my appreciation and gratitude to them as follows:

The Nithsdale Council and Dumfries Museum, for having permitted me to photograph the Kirkpatrick Macmillan bicycle; the Proprietor of the Cavendish Arms, Brindle, Lancashire, and to the Harris Museum and Art Gallery, Preston, for having granted permission to photograph 'The Brindle Battle Windows' and one of the 'Cuerdale Coins'; the Rev. D.L. Cowmeadow, of The Vicarage, Coln St. Aldwyns, Cirencester, for permitting me to copy the photograph of The Rev. John Keble, preserved in Southrop Church; John Matthews of Ainsdale, Southport, for the front cover photograph; *Bolton Evening News* for the photograph on the rear cover; Johnny Helms of Widnes, for his Foreword; the respective Editors of *Cycling Weekly* and *Cycling World* for their kind permission to include articles and photographs that have appeared in past publications.

In conclusion I should like to express my thanks to the Publisher, Alan Roby of Owl Books, Wigan.

INTRODUCTION

The reward of a leisurely and devoted pursuit of one's chosen pastime, is a deep refreshing quality of life.

The seeds are sown during life's early years; there to grow, flourish, blossom and ripen throughout youth to maturity. As the mellow days of autumn years approach, comes the fulfilment, when it is good to look back down the years and dream with reflected contentment at the bliss of treasured and stored memories. That is why I have this gratitude of life, and can rejoice and count my blessings. It has given to me over a half century of my own chosen pastime of cycle touring.

Not only that, though my scripture-allotted life span of 'three score years and ten', has come and gone, I find cycling as enjoyable as ever.

I am a happy cycling man. With my bicycle, the countryside and all nature is mine throughout the changing seasons. With advancing years, my pace is now more suited to the lazy meanders down the sun-splashed lanes that still abound. Lingering on the hidden forest ways and hollows, following the green roads and pack-horse trails and the winding and tantalising tracks and bridleways that lead to the moorlands, the fells and the high places. All of them are favourites and I love them so well.

As everyone knows, cycling in ones "veteran years" is not all sunshine — Dear Me! No! There are storms, the cold, the buffeting wind, the 'capes on' and 'capes off' days and not forgetting the wet feet. Yet there is always the 'silver lining' — the sun shining through the clouds to bring the golden glow.

I still have favourite gates and bridges to spend idle moments to lean on. I look at streams, moorland becks and rivers; I love to gaze in rapture and appreciation at the fragrance of flower-filled meadows that sweep to distant gentle hills; I sit on the friendly village green, muse on the pattern of life and watch the passing scene. There are still scores of appealing and ancient churches that speak of our Christian heritage, where I can enter and sit in the reflected peace and tranquility and try to capture the lingering echoes of a thousand yesterdays.

I talk to people on my cycling travels. There is nothing better than after exchanging the courtesies of the day with a stranger, than to indulge in good and healthy conversation on a host of topics. Such is the making of new friendships.

All these joys, though simple in character, have contributed so much to the bliss of treasured memories. They have also been shared many times with my good cycling friends and companions. Several are like me, also in their 'veteran' years. There has also been two inanimate constant good companions with me over the years, my pen and my camera. They have so faithfully recorded my feelings, impressions and cycling adventures in many ways.

In this respect, I have been flattered with the numerous requests, particularly from 'veterans of the wheel', to share these feelings, impressions and adventures in book form.

When I penned the pages of *The Golden Wheels* (now out of print) I was heartened at the response by readers, many like myself, who could recall the halcyon 'golden' years of cycling.

In response to the many requests for another volume, particularly from those who knew of my advancing years, to "do so before it is too late", I have acceded.

The old man with the white whiskers, who has been waving his scythe and hour glass at me has been given a well earned kick in the 'rear'. I have told him I am not ready yet. No, indeed, my cycling heart is still young. Turning wheels still send the adventure blood tingling and coursing through my veins.

I am pleased, therefore, to again open the pages of my 'memory book' of cycling and have gathered them together in this volume of *Golden Days Awheel*.

I hope and trust that what you read will reflect on your own happiness and enjoyment for cycling and cycle-touring and that like me, you will be able to sing its praises and applaud that sheer essence of magic it can bring.

Albert Winstanley

CONTENTS

1

Over The Hill of The Dead Men

SCENE   A remote North Yorkshire Dale in the year 1728.
SETTING   A small pack-horse alehouse favoured and frequented by itinerant traders.
CAST   Three Scottish pack-men, the Landlady of the Alehouse her daughter.
PLOT   Foul Murder.

IF you are one who is squeamish about tales of blood and murder, I would ask you not to read any further. If, on the other hand, you are of sterner quality and are prepared to risk having a ghastly nightmare and to feel your spine being tingled with terror, you are invited to join me on this ride to and over the hill of the dead men.

My introduction may at first lead you to think that this is merely a play about legend or folk lore. Let me quickly assure you it is not. It is fact and the events, I shall relate all in good time, as you join me on this cycling adventure.

At this point, you will perhaps have noticed I have not revealed the location of the story. Quite rightly so; for before the macabre there comes the magic — the magic of **Wharfedale** on a high summer's morning so happily revealed as I wheeled the bike out of the grounds of **Linton Youth Hostel**, a morning for relaxation and leisurely pedalling.

Though I have stayed overnight many times at **Linton-in-Craven**, that first greeting of the village and its green in the morning always fills me with happiness and delight. Where, for instance, can you find a village green nurtured by a prancing beck with three bridges of enhancing character, except at Linton.

The first at the top of the green, is a most ancient 'clapper' bridge of stout flat stones. This leads the eye on to the perfect specimen of pack-horse bridge, with its graceful lines and low sides. The pack-horse bridge also has a cattle ford before it. The main road bridge is but a few yards further down the beck, perhaps the 'Cinderella' of the three, but still keeping the atmosphere of it all.

There are meadow flowers there, a tall slender maypole, quaint almshouses with miniature domes. The village inn and various dwellings are grouped around as if casting friendly eyes on the green. This picture is the very essence of the Wharfedale scene.

At 8.30 a.m. there are not many people about and on this calm morning I sought the back way to **Grassington**, there to see the River Wharfe coursing beneath the town bridge. It was a bold picture, with the morning misted Grass Woods forming the background. I stopped to buy a morning paper and sweets, then it was to the back lanes again, for the eight miles or so through **Conistone village** to **Kettlewell**.

All Wharfedale was in the throes of hay-making and I had watched the busy activity on my evening ride there. Now everything was scented and a harmony of contrasting newly-cut green fields spread to the river encompassed there below. I pedalled along in happy mood, appreciating as I always do, my good fortune to be awheel in a favourite week-end dale. So far I had not thought about the grim quest that was to be my lot of the afternoon.

Coming this way in preference to the main road has many rewards. The Wharfe is revealed at its very best, you see its clarity close at hand, its curving pattern, the woodlands and water meadows. Above all in chequered display are the limestone studded fells criss-crossed by the marching stone walls that are such a feature of Craven. Nearing Kettle-well, a fine open vista sweeps from the river to Kilnsey Crag, that massive bastion that guards this part of the upper dale like a crouching lion.

All this was so pleasing. Suddenly my reverie was shattered by a resounding 'Pwang'; that sound most cyclists know that denotes a broken spoke. It was on the sprocket side and I wheeled the bike into a field for the repair. Taking the wheel out, the sprocket off, tyre and tube, all the while several sheep grouped around me viewing me quizzically as I performed with the spoke key.

Minutes later, I was in Kettlewell and saying farewell to Wharfedale, as I pedalled towards the top end of the village I knew only too well. I

Pack Horse Bridge, Linton-in-Craven.

would be having a long spell of pushing and walking before I would be saying "Hello" to **Coverdale** which was to be my way.

Each of the Yorkshire dales has its high way, connecting it with a neighbouring dale. Some can be treated as minor passes. The dales-loving cyclist knows them well and several names roll off the tongue to provide memories of the years.

The way out of Kettlewell-in-Wharfedale to Coverdale is by Park Rash, which, uncoiling like a snake, curls upwards in savage 1- in-4s. Many are the cycling stories of old when the 'Rash' was a real 'terror', especially when its surface was the roughest you could find. Since it suffered the ignominy of tarmac, the sting has been taken out of its tail; but it still commands respect and entails a good pair of lungs when pushing the bike.

Naturally, I took my time on the 'Rash', relishing the ever-opening views, with a backward glance now and then at Kettlewell rooftops. Those endearing patterned limestone walls ever marching up to distant contours. A cattle-grid marked the summit and I prepared for the fast descent that would follow to Coverdale.

I always find Coverdale a choice little dale, constantly producing little delights to tempt me out of the saddle and to 'nose' around. Today, as in Wharfedale, the emphasis was on hay-making with the fields looking so refreshing and clean. The heady scent was so strong as to make my descent sheer joy. I am so glad I do not suffer from hay-fever.

All too soon it seemed there appeared the turning I was seeking to the dominating tops on my right, with the little road bearing the sign 'Arkleside Only'. This would be my way out of the dale and to the high solitudes of a pack-horse way that is a veritable gem to those who love the treasured links with yesterday. "Better get something to eat" I told myself "before you go up there". As **Horsehouse village** was only a hundred yards or so away, I decided Arkleside could wait for a spell, and accordingly I parked the bike outside the inn that caters so well for Horsehouse.

With a healthy pint-size glass by my side and good wholesome food on the table, I was well contented. Receiving nods of welcome from the village men around the bar, I listened with interest to their talk, the main topic being hay-making and who had and who hadn't gathered the bumper crop in. Yes, indeed, in these swinging days of the '80s and '90s there is still congenial atmosphere to be found in a countryside village inn. Still subjects and topics that could well grace a masterly pen such as cycling artist Patterson could portray.

Two new things I learned about Horsehouse too, was the name of its church St. Botolph's a name linked with a 7th century saint from East Anglia and that it was a Miles Coverdale who had first translated the Bible into the English language.

A few turns of the pedals and I was turning to 'Arkleside Only' to cross over the River Cover, to reach the 'Tom Thumb' hamlet that rejoices under this name that rings with a Scandinavian flavour. I disturbed the farm dogs to reach a gate. On opening it there was my pack-horse trail steadily climbing to waiting windy heights where I should look down on **Nidderdale**, my third dale of the day.

Of the many pack-horse ways I have traversed in my long years awheel, this is one of the very best. It begins rough and twisting but slowly there comes the green and on the way to the moor top the trail is arrow straight.

I find it so easy, when on such a trail, to wheel and ride the bike in a dream. My feet and wheels now ringing the stones, now cushioned by the sheep-cropped turf. I see in my mind's eye those pack animals of long ago and the hardy pack-men who led them. There would be 'trains' of up to 20 horses, the leading animals with ringing neck bells.

This afternoon I had this pack-horse trail to myself, taking my time over it and loving every minute. I watched Coverdale slowly slip into the haze. I listened to the sign of the breeze in the grass and rushes, laughed at the sheep running from my approach and looked with interest at shapely Little Whernside on my right, topping the summit and making a dominant landmark.

When I had gained the top, I found I could ride for a spell, but on reaching a gate, I could see the trail ready to make its giddy plunge down to Nidderdale, and I knew I would be walking and coaxing the bike along for the surface would be deeply scored and rutted with water channels.

Coming into view now were the twin reservoirs of Nidderdale, the Angram and the Scar House, which all too soon capture the River Nidd in its infancy, and I could also see the two great dams that straddle the upper dale.

Slowly I manoeuvred the bike down and down to the dale, to eventually reach a level but rough road that would take me alongside the Scar House reservoir to the eventual floor of the dale.

At this stage of my story, I shall refer my reader to the beginning where I have set out the scene of what took place in the dale on a fateful day in 1728.

Over from Arkleside in Coverdale, just as I had done today, three Scots pack-men with their animals had traversed the trail, and like me, they had looked down with pleasure to Nidderdale. For them the scene was more than welcome, for down in the dale, waiting to offer hospitality was a friendly pack-horse inn, where the landlady and her daughter were well known for catering for the needs of pack-men.

Once there they left the horses to graze. Most probably a most convivial evening followed with plenty of good food and ale. This happy state of affairs continued until a later hour, by which time the pack-men were happy to sleep it all off. Throughout the evening, the landlady and her daughter had cast envious eyes on the full purses and choice goods carried by the pack-men. So much so, they decided to murder them. The foul deed was committed and the brutality was such, that the heads were severed from the bodies.

There follows a grim picture of the landlady and daughter burying the three heads and bodies on the rising hillside above the inn; and strangely they lived with the memory of their deed for some time.

Naturally the pack-men were missed and enquiries were made by fellow pack-men using the trail. The inn was still a popular calling place. On another night a pack-man happened to overhear the landlady and her daughter making plans to murder him when he was asleep. The alarm was then given.

Records are hazy as to what followed. There is an entry in the village records of Middlemoor village of how on "30th May 1728, three murdered bodies, without heads" were found. Ever since that day, the hill with its gruesome memory became known as 'Dead Man's Hill' and is so marked on the Ordnance Survey map.

The hill loomed above me as I rode the bike slowly along the stony surface of the track in its shadow and I thought about the story, and could not repress a shudder.

Even so, the hill made the prettiest of pictures in the pleasance of this late afternoon, with its varied shades of green. It blended so well as a sheltering backcloth to the Scar House reservoir. At the foot of the reservoir I could see the ornamented wall of the dam and over it I would be passing very shortly to **Ramsgill** where I had reserved accommodation for the night.

Weeks previous to my search for the story of Dead Man's Hill, I had been in correspondence with the vicar of Middlesmoor church. The result had been a letter from a historian of Nidderdale, who acquainted me with the interesting news that the former inn now lay in ruins, but described where I should find it. That is why on reaching the foot of Scar House, I continued down a private road to eventually see not the ruins as I had expected but a sturdy and neat cottage at High Woodvale.

Unfortunately there was no one at home, but with my interest thoroughly roused, I proceeded further down the rough road to a farm, and there I was greeted by the farmer. After hearing my story he smiled saying: "Aye that's it, it used to be in ruins and was built up".

Everything now seemed to be clicking into place, in my quest for the story of the Dead Man's Hill but there was one last remaining link to find. On cycling over the dam at Scar House, I 'nosed' out the beginning of another old pack-horse way, a little distance along the banks of the reservoir and by the side of a copse of trees. The map told me this would take me high above the moors on a thrilling back way to **Middlesmoor village**. It was there in the churchyard the three headless bodies were interred after being discovered on Dead Man's Hill.

A strange silence prevailed as I walked the bike overhung in places by shattered great rocks. Each twist and turn opened up breath-taking vistas of Nidderdale, the two reservoirs and the looming mass of Dead Man's Hill, which I now felt I knew so well. This ancient way I followed would be the self-same one the unhappy cortege took bearing their grim burdens in 1728.

At the summit the track linked with a walled road, extremely rough and stone strewn. With extreme care I pedalled slowly along to eventually reach Middlesmoor, the highest of the Nidderdale villages.

Fascinating is this little compact village of the dale offering a friendly atmosphere and a most intricate maze of hidden nooks and corners. I had been here before, but how happy I was to make new discoveries. I walked the bike down twisting little passages of cobbles and time-worn stone pavements and then down to the church, which seems to shyly hide itself on a hill spur overlooking the dale.

The door was open and I entered to tranquility inside. As always happens I knew a good half hour would pass by before I would leave. Inside a lovely village church I often lose myself in the spell and atmosphere that epitomises the treasured remembrances of the past. English country life is vividly portrayed and each church offers its own special contribution to our Christian inheritance.

St. Chad's church of Middlesmoor was consecrated in 1484 by "Drummond the Archbishop of York, who came riding through the Forest of Middlesmoor, with a choir of men to perform the rite".

Near this interesting inscription was a fine stone cross, with part of another at its base. This I learned had been used by St. Chad who was the Bishop of Lichfield in AD 664 to preach his sermons by.

I liked the three soaring archways of the main aisle and the several fine stained glass windows but unhappily I could not find any reference to Dead Man's Hill. My search of the churchyard failed also to reveal where the unhappy story had ended, but then it was so long ago.

Just as I had laboured up those rearing 1-in-4s of Park Rash during the morning, so was I now to thrill to the descent to **Lofthouse village** by similar 1-in-4s. Warily I tested both brakes before letting the bike 'go' on this final few miles of my adventure.

I reached level roads again to pedal the dale down towards Ramsgill and it was good to see the River Nidd at my side after its long capture in the resevoirs. I was musing about my adventures of the day and thinking about many things when suddenly the most exciting of thoughts came to me.

To explain what I mean, just glance at Sheet 91 of the Ordnance Survey map and focus your eyes on Ramsgill. There you will see the most tantalising of a double dotted line leading to Fountains Earth and up there too in bold letters you will find "Jenny Twigg and her daughter Tib".

Now I had been to see Jenny and her daughter years before, and found them to be two isolated and grotesque rocks standing sentinel on the moor. My enquiries in the dale had failed to find out the reason for their strange names but now I knew.

Most certainly the names of the evil landlady and her daughter who had murdered the three pack-men on Dead Man's Hill had been Jenny and Tib Twigg and the people of the dale had named the two rocks after them as a grim memorial of it all.

As I rode the bike towards Ramsgill for my night's stay in the dale, I knew that next morning I would just have to try and find out all about it. I told myself: "Here we go again Albert".

Jenny Twigg and her daughter Tib.

2

The Seven Wonders of Wales

WHEN I was a schoolboy (Gosh, was it so long ago?), a favourite 'general knowledge' question was: "Name the Seven Wonders of the World". At that time, I could answer immediately but now, I have to refer to my 'bumper', encyclopaedia, which gives the answer.

The 'seven wonders' are all connected with the ancient world and could very well be brought up-to-date. Why not then ask for the 'Seven Wonders of England', Scotland, or Ireland — which between them can muster seven wonders, although perhaps modesty precludes them from doing so!

Not so the Welsh. So proud of their rich historical heritage, their traditions and legends, their beautiful valleys, hills and mountains, where scenic delights and enchantments abound.

Yes, indeed, ask anyone who hails from Wales. With a proud look they will reel off a centuries-old jingle:

> *Pistyll Rhaiadr and Wrexham Steeple,*
> *Snowdon's mountain without its people,*
> *Overton yew-trees, St. Winefred's Wells,*
> *Llangollen Bridge and Gresford Bells.*

I was musing about all this as I sat at ease in the comfortable Common Room of **Ffestiniog Youth Hostel**, when homeward bound from what had been a perfect Welsh tour. I was browsing over the map, even though my plans had been made long before. I had even thought of 'Welsh Wonders' — it was a treat I had promised myself. I wanted to climb Snowdon again.

9

Three times I had climbed the mountain and by three different routes — the 'morrow would make a fourth time and by a different way. I was happy and enthusiastic with it all, for my climb to the summit of the mountain king of Wales would be the perfect finale to my tour. In this contented mood a most exciting thought began to build up — I jumped up from my chair to spread two linking maps out on the table, much to the concern of other Common Room users. I could have shouted "Eureka" — for I had discovered I could quite easily visit all of the Seven Wonders of Wales on my homeward way. In fact I would make it a 'Seven Wonder Wander'.

So lovely was the morning. Feathery silvered clouds riding a sky of speedwell blue and the sun climbing high above the peaks of Snowdonia. The morning was sheer perfection and it was all mine as I pedalled towards the first quest of the day. All nature moved in the spirit of this rich Vale of Ffestiniog and its mountains. The bike was running fine, the jacket was off, and in such harmony, I congratulated myself at having been first away from from the hostel a little after 8 a.m.

I romped along to **Aberglaslyn,** stopping a few minutes on the bridge to peer down to sunbeam-dappled torrents. Then I was thumbing down to the low gears for the short climb up the wooded vale to reach **Beddgelert** — a first class centre for Snowdon seekers. I was the first morning-coffee-and-cream-bun-man in the little cottage cafe by the bridge in the village as I looked out of the window at the passing scene. But wait what was this, a skyward glance told me that the morning would change. Little patches of dark clouds were in the offing foretelling rain. A little disheartened at this fickle change but still enthusiastic about my quest, I rode towards the well known Nant Gwynant Pass, where Snowdon can be climbed by the popular Watkin Path.

At Pont Bethania there is a well appointed 'Leisure area' and I read with interest a 'potted history' about the Snowdon path — named after Sir Edward Watkin and dedicated to the public by Prime Minister Mr. Gladstone in 1892. On that occasion, Mr. Gladstone, who was then 84, climbed to the 1000 feet mark and standing atop a huge rock, made a stirring speech to the large assembled audience. Snowdon then echoed to the rousing melody of 'Land of my Fathers'.

Well, I thought if Mr. Gladstone could climb to 1000 feet at 84, I being a much younger man could quite easily do the same. Parking the bike by a convenient wall I strode determinedly upwards. Those dark clouds I had looked at over morning coffee had given way to a rain-

Gladstone Rock, Watkin Path, Snowdon. From this rock, Prime Minister Gladstone, at the age of 84, gave a stirring speech.

threatened sky. With some dismay I watched as swirling mist slowly obscured the Snowdon approach.

By the time I had reached the 'Gladstone Rock', it was raining heavily and with my cycle cape on, walking was proving uncomfortable and a little dangerous. Snowdon is a mountain to be treated with respect and as I crouched in the lee of the rock, giving as it were a silent salute to Mr. Gladstone, I decided I should have perhaps been inviting danger to continue in the mist and rain and reluctantly I returned to the waiting bike.

With the rain pelting heavily on the cape, I prepared for the long climb of the Nant Gwynant and eventually in these unsavoury conditions, swept down through Capel Curig and Betws-y-Coed. Snowdonia was

11

now being left behind and though a little sad at the conditions cheating me of my first 'wonder quest' I looked forward to the more gentle 'Berwyn Hills, to which I now pedalled.

I arrived at **Bala Youth Hostel** to find there was a bed to spare and I wondered what next morning would bring. A 7 a.m. peep through the dormitory window revealed dull grey skies again but with breakfast away and hostel chores over, I loaded the bike and pedalled towards the deep set lanes fringing the River Dee, before I sought the climb over the high Berwyns. I had scarcely been awheel ten minutes when the rain came so I stopped by a farmhouse cottage to pull the cape over my head and to put my rain cap on.

The farmer from the cottage made his appearance and after exchanging the courtesies of the day, I made reference to the fine quality of the runner beans in his garden. Now remember if you are a cyclist in a hurry in Wales in the rain, never ever stop to talk to a dedicated Welsh farmer. From runner beans, the conversation flowed to cabbages and cauliflowers and Welsh potatoes. Then with outstretched hand, he pointed to his cows and began to rhyme off their pedigrees. "Look at that one, isn't she fine? She's been bred from a French bull". "That one there is her calf". "There's a streak of Aberdeen Angus in that one" and "Aren't those Welsh Blacks lovely?"

Astride the bike, with rain dripping from my cap and down and off my nose, it became the turn of the sheep. I learned about different breeds of ewe and tup until my mind was in a whirl. I was preparing to press on the pedal when hay was mentioned and he pointed to his barn and I was told about meadow and clover hay. He was oblivious to the rain. Perhaps I should not have been such a good listener. When eventually, I said goodbye, it was to think that such good countryside conversations are added pleasures to the cycling tourist and are so in-keeping with the happy relations between town and countryman.

A few twists and turns in the lanes and the rear of the Berwyns were before me. I romped out of Gwynned to enter Powys (how confusing these boundary names) and after rain-soaked heathery horizons I dropped down to Llangynog. Hurrah! The rain was abating and after turning at Pen-y-Bont-fawr on the road to Llanrhaiadr-ym-Mochnant, I was able to doff the cap. When in the village I was pleased to find a small cafe that provided me with a sensible teapot, a piping hot pastie and two cream cakes...Mmmmm.

Opposite: *Pystyll Rhaiadr.*

Now there is no mistaking the way to Pistyll Rhaiadr, for a sign with one word "Waterfall" beckons you on from the village. It follows the boisterous river to its valley end, where the waterfall is seen pouring over the lip of a precipitous cliff that shuts the valley in. Moreover it is a 'dead-end' road of four miles although to the terrier-nosed cyclist, there is an excellent 'rough-stuff' way, up and over the Berwyns from the fall.

Before I reached the fall, I could hear its subdued roar and once there I gasped with amazement at the thrilling spectacle. Without doubt, it is the 'daddy' of Welsh waterfalls. Pouring in tumult in a fall of 100 feet to break in confusion before gathering itself for a further fall of 140 feet. There is a natural arch of rock under which the fall pours and a flight of rough steps from the road leads to a footbridge over the river and where everything is seen to advantage.

Several photographs from different angles marked my farewell to Wonder No. 2 and then it was back down the valley to see again the lanes of the Berwyns. Just as the map had said there was a tantalising side turning in Llanrhaiadr, signposted Llanarmon, up a mischievous 'one-in-six' lane I was content to push the bike.

So bewitching were these Berwyn lanes, twisting and turning in their capricious ways. Many times I would be riding high, looking beyond hedgerows at deep-set Cyms where sturdy Welsh farms nestled against back sheltering hills. Now and then I was being rewarded with the play of light and shade over meadows and bordering lattices of trees.

My lane finale came in a fine fast swoop to the Ceiriog Valley at **Llanarmon 'D.C.'** and after a pleasant ten minutes of sitting on a wall in the village centre, I continued down the valley to **Chirk,** and high-tailing it onwards to **Llangollen** for a stay at the youth hostel there.

On my way to sign in, I popped the food bag into the Members' Kitchen, there to be greeted by two lovely New Zealand girl cyclists. They readily offered me an invitation to join them for tea and cakes, which naturally I accepted as we chatted about our respective ways and the events of the day. More than lucky cyclist me!

Llangollen is a busy Welsh town, especially with such a wealth of favoured tourist attractions so close at hand. the old 'wonder' bridge over the Dee certainly steals the glory and though it serves as a lifeline connecting both sides of the town, it is always very busy with traffic. Just let anyone dare suggest altering it or constructing a modern succes-sor.

We have to go back to the 12th century for the first records of the bridge. It was widened and had an extra arch added in the mid-14th century. On several occasions, repairs and reconstruction of portions have been necessary, but always extreme skill and care has been taken to maintain its ancient character and charm.

Leaving the hostel early, I was at the bridge before the traffic had begun to build up and gained a vantage point at river level. It was good to look above the rushing river to the ancient curving arches so mellow and graceful in the early light of the morning.

There was only sparse traffic on the road down the Vale of Llangollen, and I pedalled down towards **Ruabon**. There are several little pockets of industry in the town but on its verge I turned towards the lanes again for the four miles or so I should meander to **Overton village**.

In a twinkling, it seemed I was in a pastoral landscape with broad meadows sweeping on each side and a liberal bordering of great oaks, beeches and sycamore. Grazing cows and sheep were there to enhance the quality and the theme was most satisfying. I spotted the tower of Overton church well before I pedalled into the village and I was to find the yew trees, an enduring link with the church.

Llangollen Bridge.

Overton Church, which is surrounded by magnificent yew trees.

They formed impressive avenues encircling the church and I walked round and counted them, there were twenty one. Each, to me, had its own particular character, from the ivy creepered ones to the great giant that was split into three portions, so that I could walk right through its trunk. Some of these yew trees are estimated to be a thousand years old. Some were supported by stout posts and others had been treated with preservatives, with holes and hollows protected by wire netting.

On leaving, I thought about our allotted 'three score years and ten' but a day in the life of one of these yew trees.

A few quick twists and turns and I was following a lovely back road to **Bangor-on-Dee**, where I greeted the river again. By coming this way I should approach **Wrexham** by the 'tradesman's entrance'.

I had to follow one-way traffic signs to the town centre and in the busy high street I was happy to wheel the bike along until I came to Church Street; up which I turned. There it was, sheltering behind lovely ornamental iron gates, the soaring and graceful tower of St. Giles.

The tower dates from around 1520 and the architectural magnificence is a dedication to the devotion and calling of the men who so patiently and skilfully built it. It soars 136 feet high and is surmounted by corner turrets and other carved embellishments. I stood below, letting my eye wander from its base to turret tops, looking at the stone figures of saints, kings and queens in their niches. I thought that here, is a treasured glory of Wales, a lasting symbol of our Christian inheritance. So strikingly beautiful.

Inside the church the verger greeted me warmly, giving up his time to escort me around and to point out many surprises I would otherwise have missed. He told me about Elihu Yale who lived in Wrexham and became the benefactor and founder of America's most famous Yale University. He even pointed out his tomb in the churchyard and regaled me with the story of how a replica of the church tower had been built at Yale by the Americans. Not only that, he indicated a spot on the tower from which a stone had been removed to be built into the American replica. This was a bond of friendship between Wrexham and Wales and the United States.

A mile or so away along the Chester Road was **Gresford**, where very shortly another church would command my attention in my 'wonder quest'. I had always treated Gresford as a busy little place of industry to be hurried through on my way to North Wales. Now for the very first time I was to seek out a little more of what Gresford had to offer.

My turning took me to a country lane with fields and hedgerows. There were trim attractive houses with well-kept gardens and my eye was led on to the church of All Saints and its pinnacles topping the tower. There were yew trees here also in the churchyard and I found myself eagerly looking forward to seeing more of the church, so rich in historical interest.

I left the bike by a fence and walked towards the church gates and it was with dismay I noticed the heavy padlocks on them. Two more would-be visitors made themselves known and told me of their disappointment at this turn of events. I was determined not to be cheated of my visit and was eventually directed to the vicarage.

Unfortunately there was no-one at home. A little dejected I walked back down the drive. Had I not stopped to speak to a parishioner, telling her of my quest and saying how sorry I was about the church being closed I would have missed completely the car that pulled up in the village nearby. My friendly parishioner exclaimed with laughter: "Why, there's the vicar now!"

She introduced me to him and though he was already late for his lunch proferred to show me the church, whilst regretfully explaining that unhappily, precautions had to be taken because of possible vandalism.

We entered the church by his vestry and through a beautiful 'Lady Chapel' and then he led me to the west end. Standing there he told me its most colourful story and history. A lovely feeling of tranquility was there. Reflections of yesteryears were being awakened as the vicar pointed its beauty out to me.

I thanked the vicar for his kindness and the trouble he had taken. He regretted that the verger, who had the keys to the belfry tower, was away, but there would always be a welcome to see them whenever I was in the village again.

With the bike again I took a last look at the church and tower that houses the eight bells that contribute their music to the 'Seven Wonders of Wales'. I knew that I should never be content until I had heard them ringing their peals and message music over the meadows of this Gresford corner of Wales.

Time, as always, had been passing quickly. After the lanes I knew I should have to indulge in some fast pedalling to see my last wonder — the Well of St. Winefrede at Holywell. Unfortunately I should have to suffer a spell of main road riding to get there before the 'shrine' containing the well closed for the day.

I passed through **Hope** and **Mold** and was making good time and congratulating myself when a 'snap and ping' noise from the rear told me a spoke had broken.

"It's no use", said 'Inner Man' — "You'll just have to stop and put a new spoke in or you'll only have a more buckled wheel if you don't".

I decided to take his advice, unshipping panniers and saddlebag, upending the bike and feverishly starting work on the offending wheel. Naturally it was on the 'block' side and it was a case of wheel out, block off, tyre and tube off, old broken spoke out, thread new one in, and play about with the spoke key and all the time hoping St. Winefrede would wait for me! Twenty minutes later the bike was loaded again. I hurriedly ran to a muddy pool to wash my black and oil grimed hands, much to the concern of some ducks on a nearby pond who flew away squawking in protest at the proceedings.

I did not stop again until I reached **Holywell** town and perspiring I hastened to the shrine of St. Winefrede with a half- hour to spare before 'closing time'.

The story of St. Winefrede has come down the ages from the seventh century. She was a simple village girl, who had often disdained the forced attentions of the evil 'Caradoc', the son of a neighbouring prince. There was a day when he entered the household of the girl and finding her alone, he again tried to force his attentions on her. She managed to escape from his advances and in terror, ran screaming from the house pursued by Caradoc. She was no match for him and when caught, he beheaded her in a rage just as Beuno the father of the girl made his appearance.

Beuno laid a curse on the prince, who immediately died on the spot. Where Winefrede's head had tumbled, a spring gushed out of the ground; at the self same spot it gushes from today. Prayers were immediately said by the good village people for Winefrede and by a miracle, her head was restored to her body. The only wound to be seen was a 'thin line' around her neck.

From that day, St. Winefrede as she became and the Holy Well, acquired fame. It is now a 'Welsh Lourdes' in miniature. There are many accounts of miraculous cures from ailments being enacted there and the story of long centuries of pilgrimages to the well occupy a prominent chapter in religious Welsh history.

I walked by the side of the great bath, which is used for total immersion and then I passed into the inner shrine to look at St. Winefrede in her candle-lit niche. Standing there in the silence of the shrine, and in the dim light of the flickering candles was a moving experience; the only disturbance being the noise of the gush of the water from underground. There was a tap provided to drink from the well and this I did, appreciating that such beautiful stories of faith still live on in this high pressure age of ours.

From Holywell there was a fast free-wheel down to the coast road, which I should follow, backing the shores of the Dee on my way to **Chester** for the last night of my tour. Now pedalling at my normal and sensible leisurely speed, I let my mind wander down the events of the past three days.

Mine had been the most happy of cycling quests. Mine the joy of seeking out the 'Seven Wonders of Wales'. Certainly I had not kept to the order of the rhyme, but there had been the lure and natural rhythm that had taken me through inspiring Welsh terrain. There had also been unfolded for me the delights of the mountains and valleys, the torrents and waterfalls and the churches with their history.

As I pedalled onwards towards Chester, I was repeating the old 'Seven Wonder' jingle that had set me off on the quest and though I lacked that captivating and musical lilt that only the Welsh can provide, I now knew the lines and words as well as any David, Ivor, Llewellyn or Hugh.

3

The Nine Ladies of Stanton Moor

I SHALL always remember the day I had tea and biscuits with nine ladies. Even though I arrived uninvited, they did not complain; nor did they raise any objection when I wheeled the bike over their front doorstep to lean it on the wall of their home.

It was on a morning when I had been caught up in the fascinating spell of the past and had crossed with the bike what must be the most mysterious moorland in England. That morning had given to me many rewarding memories and visible ones at that, of our ancient ancestors, so that my call for 'elevenses' on the nine ladies was in the way of an added delight.

Grey old **Elton village** in upland **Derbyshire** was the starting point for my morning ride into the past. A firm favourite with me for many years now, the old village typifies all that is most peaceful in the Derbyshire scene. The pattern of life there does not seem to change with the passing years. I like the small snug cottages of sturdy grey stone and the well-stocked village shop where you can buy anything from humbugs to bike parts.

There is a venerable old church and, of course, Elton Old Hall, to me a youth hostel of homely quality and atmosphere, which, alas, seems to be disappearing from the association these days.

At the time of which I write, the Warden had a perky pup. Cyclists were his firm favourites and he would welcome them with a bark from atop the hostel gatepost. One had to beware, for a back wheel to 'Tuck' the pup was something to be prolifically watered. Once I had to chase him after he had generously watered my saddlebag, but then, it probably served me right for leaving it unattended on the floor whilst wheeling my bike to the shed. Alas poor Tuck fell victim to a car some time ago, but I should like to think that in some doggy celestial field, Tuck will be still up to his antics!

The autumn morning was sharp and clear as I left the village to swing to my right beyond the church. With high stippled clouds and the meadows sparkling with dew, a light playful breeze to ruffle my thinning hair.

Robin Hood's Stride.

Within minutes I was walking as the lane curved upwards by **Harthill Moor**. I could, of course have maintained the hill easily with my ultra-low gears but preferred to walk just to admire the back view of Elton with that church tower topping the meadows.

Before riding again at the hilltop, I lifted the bike over a pole fence, to follow a bracken verged pathway which took me to the back door of **Mock Beggar Hall**, or as it is better known — Robin Hood's Stride, which is such a pleasing feature here of the landscape.

The 'Stride' is the name associated with the two pinnacles of soaring rock standing on top of the other tumbled rocks which are massive and of fantastic shape. The pinnacles are some 30 feet apart and between them (so they say), the hero of Sherwood could stride with ease. The men of Elton seated in their comfortable 'local' with healthy pints, will tell you another version. I shall always remember being regaled with the story of how Little John, Robin's trusted lieutenant, could quite easily stand with one leg on each pinnacle, and of how it was his favourite stance as the will and convenience took him (after pints in the local).

Back on the bike, I coasted swiftly downhill cheered with fleeting glimpses of **Youlgreave village** to my immediate left.

A sharp right turn now down by a lane took me to the main road coming up from Haddon. In a matter of minutes, I was in the lanes again with the village of **Stanton-in-the-Peak** my immediate objective. It was just 9 a.m. and so far from leaving Elton I had not seen a soul or vehicle and I relished the quiet air of peace of the autumn morning. Autumn is a wonderful time of the year in any county of countryside England and I am happy to cycle and sample the sweetness which the season brings. The growing pageantry of glowing and changing tree colour. The tyres rustling the fallen leaves and crackling over the acorns and chestnuts.

Many pheasants from the Stanton Estate were here grubbing the hedgerows and flying off at my approach. I was thrilled to watch a ding-dong battle between two mature birds, beaks flashing and feathers flying and I was almost on them before they decided to fly off.

In Stanton-in-the Peak there are convenient seats by the war memorial and facing the church. Here I had five minutes or so admiring the striking church spire and gracious oak tree in the churchyard, fully 40 feet high with not a bough for twenty feet or more. Behind me was the inn with its unusual name of 'The Flying Childers', so called, I understand from a famous racehorse.

Stanton occupies a high elevation and by looking down the village I could see the pleasing greens of patterned fields giving way to the darker greens of richly wooded Haddon Hall in the valley of the Wye.

Still walking through the village and still climbing, I took the road to **Stanton Moor** and then on my left were the first captivating views of the heath and moorland I should be exploring later in the morning. I had only been riding a short distance when across a field I could see a massive boulder ringed by a low wall. It called for investigation. On wheeling the bike there I found it to be a boulder which I should estimate to be 20 or more tons in weight.

On its side were footholds and iron handles. Naturally I had to climb to the top. It was then I saw that flash of brown — a large fox walking by a wall oblivious of my presence. I watched him moving with grace and cunning, clear the wall and vanish into dense woodland.

I came down from my boulder perch and there followed a lovely freewheel to **Birchover village,** to come to a halt by the 'Druid Inn' there. Like me there must be many who seeing a country inn with an unusual name have to seek out its story. Perhaps it is a failing but I have had many adventures when my terrier nose has decided to investigate.

The mention of Druids brought instantly to mind those men of the strange cult in their flowing white robes taking part in weird and sacrificial orgies and incantations in their rocky temples.

To add to this fantasy I found that the Inn has for its background one of the most fantastic piles of rocks I have ever seen. they stretched for some 80 yards rising to about 150 feet. They were weird and spooky and I wandered in and out of strange cave like rooms carved in the rock and it was as if long departed 'Druid' chiefs were watching my every step. I nosed into tunnels and passages and there was also a massive boulder stone some 50 tons in weight balanced alarmingly on two smaller rocks. There were also carved seats and 'armchairs' for the 'Elders'.

When I returned from my visit, I discovered I should have paid a modest admission fee. Ah well, never mind, I had had excellent value.

It is fitting that in the midst of such Druidical fantasy and surroundings that Birchover should possess such a gem as the little church that nestles down a lane in the shadow of the Druid Rocks. The door was open when I entered and there was the lovely scent of flowers waiting to be arranged for Harvest Festival.

I learned that the church was built by a Thomas Eyre around 1700 but I could not repress a shudder when I read that he built it "in recompense for practising Black Magic".

The armchairs for the 'Elders' at the Druid Rocks, Birchover.

There were delightful paintings of carved fruit on the pew ends and a wonderful carved pulpit and alms boxes. As I placed a contribution in the box, I read with interest the notice over it:

> *Notice to Louts . . . the boxes in this church are*
> *cleared every day. It won't be worth your while*
> *to break them open for your beer money, as there won't*
> *be much in (if anything) — so don't put yourself*
> *to the trouble.*

A sad reflection, I thought, on the acts of vandalism we have to put up with these days.

I retraced my way to the top end of the village and followed the sign in ancient lettering pointing to Stanton Moor.

The moor takes its place as one of the wonders of Britain. Barrows, burial chambers, cairns and mysterious standing stones and circles are there in plenty. Archaeologists have over the years, and are still patiently gleaning the story of the large community of Bronze Age dwellers who peopled the moor in the twilight of our early island story.

There are also great rocks and stones of weird shape, similar to the one I had climbed earlier and naturally named accordingly, like the Cat Stone, the Cork Stone, the Druids Seat and Crown Stone.

The soft morning sunshine burnished the varying colours of bracken and bilberry bordering the pathway I was riding along and in the lonely spell and solitude of this mysterious high domain, pure autumn harmony prevailed.

Here were the timeless echoes of an ancient past — memories of men who were the forerunners of our civilization; men who had raised their crops and children, who had grazed their cattle and who had left behind them these strange relics. They were too, I am sure, men who loved the countryside and cherished the passing seasons as we do today.

At one point I stopped to look at a few trees that grew together from a heap of stones. When I examined the stones, I could see a pattern. They had obviously been arranged by long-forgotten hands. Perhaps, I thought, the trees with branches reaching to the light and the sky had roots deeply embedded in some crumbled bone remains of those ancestors of old.

The pathway was easy to ride along. Then peeping through the trees and topping the moor, I saw a tall square tower making quite an impressive picture in the morning sunshine. On it was carved a crown and the words, Earl Grey 1832. This tower was built to commemorate the Reform Act and is used to afford a wonderful view of the moor. Unhappily on account of vandalism the door has had to be bricked up.

A few yards on I saw a branching track, leading to the tree shade. This I followed eagerly wheeling the bike, my excitement was mounting all the time. Yes, they were there peeping at me over the top of the low wall of their home — the Nine Ladies of Stanton Moor.

How well they were looking in the filtered sunshine, their faces turned towards me in the quiet of their lonely abode. Each lady was ranged almost equidistant from her sister, although each had a different standing and bearing.

I wheeled the bike into their home and I went towards them. When in the centre I decided this was a good place for 'elevenses' and that is how I had tea and biscuits with the nine ladies!

Admittedly it was a little eerie sitting there in the silence with the 'ladies' looking on. Mute as they were, they could tell me a story of those twilight days of history. The Nine Ladies of Stanton Moor make a perfect example of early Bronze Age Stone Circle and it is the finest monument on the moor. It is some 35 feet in diameter and dates back to about 1500

B.C. It was certainly used in connection with religious worship. Only yards away and keeping his eye on them, whilst all on his own is the King Stone.

The little pathway was now circling me back towards my starting point. I rode high over the moor and then, glory be, there was another huge rock with hand and footholds just simply asking to be climbed. This I did and happily rested a few minutes sitting in a perfectly shaped 'Druid Chair' in a rock facing.

A few yards further on I reached tarmac and the road back to Stanton-in-the-Peak.

It was a more than wonderful freewheel back towards the village with the fingers handy on the brake levers in the ecstacy of the descent. The sun was still there, high climbing the autumn sky, the bracken and tree colours and the breeze tingling my cheeks and legs. Yet there are those who say this cycling touring pastime of ours is dying out. Rubbish, I say. Let them seek out these countryside lanes. Better still let them come with me sometime in the future with their bikes to have morning tea and biscuits with Nine Ladies.

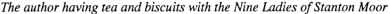

The author having tea and biscuits with the Nine Ladies of Stanton Moor

POSTSCRIPT:

A short time ago I returned to pay my respects to the Nine Ladies. To my regret they had lost the protecting wall of their home and looked so forlorn and lonely in their woodland setting. The King Stone too did not seem to have his former regal bearing. It did not seem as comfortable and cosy with my flask and biscuits. I do sincerely hope that nothing untoward or sinister will happen to them. After all, such ancient remains must be preserved and their stories handed down to those who will follow.

4
"He Builded Better Than He Knew"

ON a day in 1842, a young Scottish blacksmith faced the magistrates in the courtroom at Dumfries. He had been charged with negligence following a most unfortunate accident, when he had knocked down a young girl on the Queen's highway.

He was found "Guilty", and in his stern voice, the presiding magistrate warned him to be more careful in future . . . and "You will be fined, Sir, the sum of five shillings".

Little did he know that the sentence and fine imposed upon him would take its place in British cycling history — as being the very first time a cyclist had appeared before a Court, and had been fined.

The blacksmith was Kirkpatrick Macmillan, the inventor of the first bicycle to be seen in Britain — and you can capture the memory of it all, as well as see a perfect replica of the machine, in the town museum at **Dumfries**. Moreover, having seen it, you can then cycle lovely by-lanes from Dumfries to **Keir Mill village**, where Macmillan lived and carried on his trade. The old smithy where the story began is still very much there.

We were bound for the Scottish Highlands, having travelled from our Lancashire

This centenary plaque was placed on the wall of the Old Smithy at Keir Mill, near Dumfries, in 1939, to honour Kirkpatrick Macmillan

hometowns to Dumfries by train. With time to spare, I remembered being told that the 'Macmillan Bicycle' could be seen in the town museum. To us, it would be a lovely introduction to our tour. Enquiring at the Tourist Information Centre in Dumfries, we were told that the museum was not far away. My companions readily followed as I led the way.

We found the museum in the same building as the 'Camera Obscura', the forerunner of photography, which is a well-known attraction for visitors and were readily granted permission to proceed to an upper floor, where in company with other early machines, the Macmillan bicycle held pride of place.

Up to 1840, the 'hobby horse' had held sway, being propelled by the legs straddling the wooden frame. The young blacksmith, after many experiments, succeeded in connecting the rear wheel to the front by rods with 'pedals' at the end, and sitting confortably on his saddle, the hard work of the 'hobby horse' was at an end.

Naturally he became the object of much attention pedalling the strange machine around the nearby lanes, and sometimes caused much

Below: *The Old smithy, Keir Mill, where the first British bicycle was invented.* **Inset:** *Commemorative plaque on wall of smithy.*

IN THIS SMITHY
THE FIRST BICYCLE
WAS BUILT BY THE
INVENTOR

KIRKPATRICK M^CMILLAN
ABOUT THE YEAR
1840

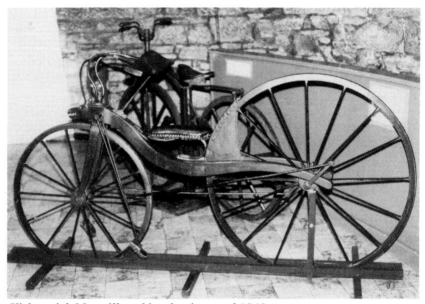

Kirkpatrick Macmillans bicycle - invented 1840.

consternation at the speed at which he could travel. I suspect it was curiosity that had caused the young girl to run into his path. He knocked her down, which resulted in his court appearance and fine.

Looking at the machine, it was easy to picture those first cycling days of long ago, and I knew I should just have to go to Keir Mill to see the 'Old Smithy' where the invention had been made.

The Dumfries highway was not to our liking. It was with some relief that we turned to the lanes to eventually arrive in the village. There it was, the Old Smithy, now converted into a pleasing end cottage. There were white walls, and a green sward fronting the cottage. What is more, there was an ancient water pump with flowers occupying the stone trough before it.

It was easy to picture the scene of long ago, of impatient horses outside the smithy waiting to be shod, the sound of the hammer on the anvil, the glowing forge, the blacksmith taking the red hot shoes and beating them into shape.

I could picture a 'hobby-horse' leaning on the wall outside and in idle moments, the blacksmith pondering on how he could improve it, until

"Eureka!"... the problem was solved and the very first British bicycle was born.

In 1939, on the occasion of the centenary of the bicycle, a plaque was placed in position on the smithy wall by The National Committee on Cycling, to honour the memory of the inventor. This kept company with a smaller plaque recording the invention.

To have seen the replica of the very first bicycle in Britain, and to have seen where it was invented, was the perfect introduction to our tour. I particularly liked also, the sentence stating : "He Builded Better Than He Knew" for Patrick Macmillan certainly did just that!

5

Journey to the Island of Valencia

WHEN I was a small boy, there was no such thing as the 'Top of the Pops' or 'The Top Ten'. The 'numbers' of the day were of equal merit and their popularity was such that the words and melodies were on everyone's lips.

We had dreamy and sentimental ballads, love songs, lively refrains, and there was also a glut of rousing choruses that we all sang with gusto.

One I particularly remember was 'Valencia', and even today, in my mature years, I can give a fair bathroom rendering of "VA...LEN...CI...A" — land of orange groves and sweet content, you call me from afar . . .". After this first line, I usually receive a shout to "Shut up!"

In that boyhood age 'Valencia', with that long drawn out first word, was to be heard everywhere. The cycling butcher, baker, and newspaper boy whistled it as they pedalled their heavy delivery bikes. Tram drivers, milkmen, rag-and-bone men and a host of other street traders bellowed it out. Dogs of every pedigree barked joyfully on hearing it. Alley cats purred with affection at the sound and not to be outdone, every horse pulling a cart along the high street seemed to have dancing feet, as the melody and words swept across the land.

When the joys of cycling began to be kindled in my young heart, whilst riding my first heavy 'sit-up-and-beg' bike, I too sang 'Valencia'. I would picture distant shores of Spain and all the delights of that land, around which the song was centred. In my boyhood ambition, I said: "I shall go there one day!"

Now the scene changes to these my veteran years, when I can look back on four thrilling and adventure-packed cycle tours of Spain. Yet I never did manage to visit Valencia to revive my boyhood song.

Nevertheless, I have been to Valencia and if this sounds 'Irish' to you, it is indeed so. For Valencia is also the name of a small island cheekily thrusting itself into the Atlantic ocean, a stone's throw from the coast of **Kerry.**

My going there only came about as the result of a casual remark and but for same, I should not have the happy memories I now treasure of the little place.

It all came about when in the company of three touring companions of long standing. We were en route for the noted Ring of Kerry. A week of pelting rain and high winds had buffeted us; every day had been all grey and gloom. Our touring spirits were definitely at a low ebb, as we had so looked forward to seeing those majestic peaks, the MacGilly-cuddy's Reeks, and to penetrate with our wheels, their elusive tracks and paths. Instead they had all been dressed in grey shrouds, swept by stinging rain.

We had come coastwards, hoping things would be better, yet it seemed Ireland had borrowed cold days from November, presenting them in a high summer of July to us. Wet, cold and miserable we had followed the Ring of Kerry way down to **Cahersiveen,** where during the mid-afternoon we had decided to replenish our supplies for the coming camp for the night. As we squelched our way into the shops, there was some good-humoured blarney and banter, with my good friend Steve pointing to the weather and saying: "What's it like here in the summer?" "To be shure, 'tis not like this always", came the reply.

After passing through Cahersiveen, the Ring of Kerry makes a sweep over a high peninsula and down to Waterville; and this should have been our way. In the dull weather our eyes were on the lanes and we made a swing to the coast again, backing the Portmagee Channel. It was along here, being pounded still by the strong wind, that something most welcome began to take place. First the rain decided to stop and the grey clouds began to be silvered. We stopped to shake the capes, roll them and strap them to the saddlebags. Steve, obviously now in a happier mood, in the most nonchalant and casual manner pointed to a side-turning and said: "The bridge to Valencia is down there". I pricked up my ears, Valencia, I had never given the island a thought and here we were merely a stones-throw away. "Right, we're going", I said and immediately the song of my boyhood rang out on that Irish lane. The other three were not too happy about spending a night there but seeing my mind was made up, they meekly followed as I turned my wheels towards the island.

Within a hundred yards or so, a fitful sun had beamed through the clouds, sending faint gleams on the turbulant waters of Portmagee Channel that separates the island from the Kerry shores; this was surely a good omen of welcome for the short stay we now all eagerly looked forward to.

We approached the trim little coastal village of Portmagee which made a pretty picture with several fishing boats bobbing in the heavy harbour swell, and the splash of differing colours of the dwellings seen against the harbour waves enhanced the sea vista. Forgotten now was the rain though still tormenting us was the wind blowing in fury from the Atlantic. As we reached the bridge it was as if unseen hands were trying to prevent us from crossing to the island.

Valencia Island, has, of course, been served by ferry for many years from Knightstown. Perhaps the building of the bridge from Portmagee has stolen some of the magic away with access now being so easy. Still it is not every day that one can cycle across a bridge over the Atlantic and despite the wind there was that feeling of excitement as we pedalled the last few yards to reach the island.

The island is only a small one — a mere seven miles long by three wide and served by good roads. The average fast pedalling cyclist who rarely stops, could well easily complete the circuit in 'under-the-hour'.

The bridge over the Atlantic to Valencia Island.

Yet, for the dedicated tourist who pedals his quiet way, the island is spiced with many good things and offers some spectacular cliff scenery.

There is an unfolding pattern of small fields and meadows of snug cottages of white and thatch which are so endearing and typical of the traditional Irish landscape. Hardy island sheep and cows graze the headlands and here and there you bump into an Irish donkey, without which no Irish scene is complete. A point of interest is that the island acquired fame in 1858 when it became the terminal for the first transatlantic cable from Newfoundland.

Our first concern was for a spot to camp. On crossing the bridge we had noticed a disused coastguard station facing the channel, the lee side of which would make an admirable spot. Fortunately we were to meet the new owner who had bought the property for development. He readily gave us permission to camp behind it. Once the tents were up and sheltered from the wind, we began that most pleasurable of camp chores, preparation of the evening meal.

As always we dined well. Part of the sweet course was a Spanish orange each, just to put the finishing touch to it all. Our earlier flagging touring spirits had been considerably uplifted.

This happy state of affairs, however, was not to last long. The persistent wind was bringing the rain again and once the camp chores were over it was 'inside the tents' and shut out the storm.

Warm and snug in my sleeping bag and in the light from my candle, I opened the map and looked at the little island marked there 'Valencia', on which we were camped. I could hear the waves pounding into surf on the channel shores of the Atlantic and the wind moaned eerily in the many corners and nooks of the roofless building. Now and then a squall of rain would beat a tattoo on the nylon flysheet.

Naturally, as is so often a habit with me, I fell to dreaming about the adventures of the day and the song that had brought us here.

The morning came fitful and grey. The raucous scream of seagulls, flying and dipping over the channel, challenged the wind. Not to be outdone scores of jackdaws then added their protests at the wind.

The rain had now stopped and in good heart we prepared for what the day and the island had in store for us.

In the grey of the island morning, we butted into the wind, the low gears in play, steadily climbing towards Bray Head, the southernmost point of the island. This marked the point where we should turn our wheels inland and across the island. But before doing so we parked the bikes to walk the headlands; for the Ordnance map denoted in ancient letters the word 'Fort'.

We tramped the rough and rain-soaked headland, looking at the remains of historic tumbled walls, strange mounds and hollows and approached as far as we dared, the cliff tops, to peer down at the turmoil and confusion below. That bitter wind was providing us with the most thrilling of spectacles. Down there massive Atlantic breakers were pounding ceaselessly at the cliffs, hurling themselves into destruction and sending spumes and dense white spray to the grey mist.

It was ocean savagery at its best, yet this wind-pounded headland on which we walked was a veritable mosaic of colour, with flowers of varying hues; how we longed for the sunshine which would have revealed it all so bright and sparkling.

On the bikes again, it was time to exchange seaward Valencia for the backbone of the island, and the now easy road that would eventually take us to **Knights Town** the largest place there. From this 'spine' we were able to look down on the island scene, dipping towards the Portmagee Channel and despite the dull morning, a landscape of serene mellowness was revealed. The endearing character of patterned fields was there, the trim little farmsteads of white and thatch, the varying hues of the flowers and the contrasting greens. Here also were the sturdy island cattle and sheep grazing peacefully, and there was that lovely feeling that life here goes on a much slower and contented way.

A rough lane making for the sea headlands attracted our attention, and we just had to go and see where it led. We followed it to its end, and then tramped over a rough terrain to the foothills looking to the high Fogher Cliffs.

Just as we had watched the spectacle of the Atlantic breakers at Bray Head, so now we were to be treated to a still more thrilling display, more so as the fierce wind added to the excitement. Yet we had to take extreme care, as a sudden loss of foothold on the cliff tops in the wind could easily have meant oblivion!

On the bikes again, we continued riding the island 'back-bone' now skirting the northern shores. Again it was a minor road with a sign 'Grotto' that caused us to turn aside to follow the beckoning way. We found the road was taking us high above the coast with Valencia Harbour down below as we approached a large disused slate quarry.

Slate quarries are not exactly things of scenic quality, and are usually eyesores. This one, however, was to present a rare surprise. It came when we turned a corner and saw the great black yawning mouth of the quarry

A lane near Fogher, Valencia Island.

before us. Instead of the usual untidy morrain, everything was neat and tidy. We were surprised to find railings at the entrance enclosing a lovely tinkling fountain. Before it was a memorial stone to a past priest of Valencia, who had erected the grotto and the whole was in the form of a shrine.

In a niche high above the grotto entrance was a statue of the Madonna. Thoroughly pleased with our discovery, we retraced our way and now the magnificent panorama of the coast was ideally revealed. We could see the larger island of Beginish as well as many rock-ribbed islets being pounded and thrashed by those Atlantic waves. There was even spasmodic sunshine sending stippled lightbeams dancing over the water.

All too soon it was gone as we came to a dense wooded area hiding the view and we prepared for the remaining mile or so to Knights Town, with almost a gale chilling us to the bone. How we welcomed the piping hot tea at the first cafe we approached and the meal that followed as we sat round the table thawing out and talking about the events of the morning.

Knights Town caters for the visitors to Valencia, and there is also a conveniently placed youth hostel. I liked too, the massive anchor in the town that has been renovated and serves as a memorial.

On our way again, we were now down to sea level, on the fast road backing the Portmagee Channel. Again it was a most intimate landscape that was presented, with the sweeping views of the channel and the mainland, the flower tangled hedgerows, the fuschia and other creepers and the now familiar chequered pattern of the fields.

There was a twist and turn to enter **Chapeltown**, next in importance to Knights Town, and an equally twist and turn out again to the coast road.

Over on the mainland now, we could see Portmagee, still as attractive and colourful as it had been yesterday. We gave a silent salute to the disused coastguard station that had served us so well overnight and then the 'Bridge over the Atlantic' was there to take us off the island.

I was thoroughly happy and decided to treat myself to a personal farewell rendering of the song:

"Land of orange groves and sweet content, you call me from afar . ."

After all, I was well behind the other three, or I should have received a "Shut-up"!

Despite the weather the sweet content was there and I knew that I could be back one day to see again the little island with its flowers, its inland charm and dramatic cliff scenery but I would go when preferably everything was bathed in sunshine.

I was alone when I stopped by the little harbour on the mainland at Portmagee for a final picture and glancing towards the high hill of the Ring of Kerry was before me, it was to see the dark gathering storm clouds on the tops again.

Halfway up the hill, the other three were waiting for me, chastising me for the delay and yet I had to treat myself to a last look at Valencia Island disappearing into the grey and gloom.

POSTCRIPT:

There may be some readers of this narrative who may question my spelling of the island, saying it should be 'Valentia'. We were following sheet 20 of the Irish Ordnance Survey - Suirbheireacht Ordonais (Dingle Bay) which names the island — 'Valencia'. So there!

6

The Buried Treasure of Cuerdale

I AM sure that the mere mention of buried treasure is sufficient to send the hot blood tingling down the veins of most boys, including their dads and grandads.

I have a story of buried treasure to relate and though it does not have the romantic and traditional island setting, it is one that is unique in our history. Moreover, though I love the fictional story of Treasure Island, Long John Silver and his parrot, not forgetting Jim Hawkins, my 'treasure' is fact and the setting is my native Lancashire.

On most Sunday mornings there is a steady passage of cyclists passing through the town of Preston. You see the bright coloured jerseys of the racing men 'honking' up the steep hill from Walton-le-Dale and over the Ribble bridge to the town. There are men on 'fixed' and others with multigearing, tandems, and 'barrow boys'. There are also the dedicated veteran tourists, who walk the hill on their way to the elusive Lancashire lanes of the Fylde, or the many waiting delights of the **Ribble Valley**.

On such a Sunday morning I was alone and in meditative mood as I walked the Walton-le-Dale hill and had cast an admiring glance at the Ribble, looking over to the spread of green. It was the sort of morning for lazily turning the pedals for leisure and lingering by riverside banks. I knew immediately what I would be doing. Instead of passing through Preston I decided to curve my way to the next bridge up-river. From there follow the downward flow and complete a circuit back to Walton-le-Dale.

Twenty or more years had passed since I had followed this particular Ribble reach, walking and riding the river banks.

At the top of Walton hill I turned towards the Salmesbury Blackburn highway, knowing that I should soon be seeing the Ribble again at

Brockholes Bridge, which in years past was the haunt of badgers. Today no sensible badger would dream of building a 'sett' there, for the highway is usually choc-a- bloc with fast moving traffic.

When I reached the bridge, I was so glad to see that the little pathway that dipped down to the river banks was still there. In a twinkling I was wheeling the bike by the side of the Ribble. Now riding, now walking with the bike, I was as happy as the proverbial sandboy.

The prosperous looking farm I was soon to pass was Cuerdale Hall Farm. On passing through a gateway, the pathway now grass covered, I found myself looking for something I remembered was there 20 years before. It was still there — a sturdy stone pillar sitting above the river banks.

I leaned the bike by its side, spread my cape on the grass, and sitting there over my flask and a chocolate bar, I reconstructed the scene that took place here in the 10th century.

In the early years of that turbulent century, marauding Vikings had subdued almost the whole of England, except Wessex, where good King Alfred (when he was not burning cakes) ruled supreme. He was succeeded by his golden haired grandson, Athelstan. In AD 937 history records the Battle of Brunanburg with Althelstan taking part. It was a fierce encounter that was destined to change our history. Before and after Brunanburg, there were skirmishes with the Vikings in many part of England and a particular fierce one was fought here on these sweeping plains of the Ribble. Again the name of Athelstan is linked with it.

Anluf the Dane (chief of the 'baddies') had gathered a large invading force from Ireland, with allies from the Scots and the Welsh and their longships were anchored in the estuary of the Ribble. The invading Vikings then sailed up the river, which in those days was navigable and came ashore in these fields and meadows of Cuerdale. Athelstan and his brother Edmund the Atheling were here.They were commanding the main body of the waiting English army (the 'goodies') and in the ensuing battle the Vikings were easily routed. The remnants of the defeated forces hurriedly retreated to the Ribble, to sail down river to their anchored fleet. As a result of this victory, Athelstan was acclaimed all over Europe. The Viking rule in England was ended. For the very first time in our island's history, a single monarch ruled.

Unhappily, Athelstan did not enjoy this peace for long, for he was to die in AD 940.

Sitting on these Ribble banks on this sun-splashed Sunday morning, I could picture the scene — the noise and tumult of battle, the clash of swords, the screams and shouts of the dying. Vikings in their winged battle helmets brandishing embellished shields as they hurriedly jumped into their boats to try and escape the deadly hail of English spears.

Now, where I was sitting, was the actual spot where a buried treasure was discovered . . . a treasure that was to link itself with the battle. Amazingly there was an interval of almost 1000 years between the two events.

On 15th May, 1840, a gang of workmen were working here, making repairs to the river banks to counteract erosion, when to their surprise their spades struck something solid. Carefully they dug round the buried object and slowly they unearthed a massive leaden chest. When opened it contained between 7,000 and 10,000 valuable coins. There were also silver ingots and rare items of personal charms and adornments. When the coins were examined, they were found to cover the periods of our history previous to AD 937; most of them minted in the reigns of the Kings of Mercia.

The only explanation, according to the experts, was that this was 'battle plunder' taken by the Vikings. Being unable to take it back during their retreat to the boats on the Ribble, they buried it on the river bank. Obviously they intended to come back

Right: *This stone marks the site of the 'Cuerdale Hoard', buried by Vikings in AD937. The 'Hoard' was discovered in a lead chest in 1840.* **Below:** *A Saxon coin discovered at the site.*

for it at a later date but history decided otherwise.

As for the stone erected to mark this important spot, it bears the carved inscription: "Site of Cuerdale Hoard 15 May 1840". Some of the coins can be seen in Preston museum.

Soon having completed the riverside pathways, I was approaching Walton-le-Dale again with the squat tower of the church there, making the prettiest of pictures overlooking the tree clad banks of the river.

A farm lane brought me out at the village, and it was strange to feel tarmac again, as I turned towards the maze of little lanes I know so well in this area, promising myself a glass at the village inn at **Brindle**. The Cavendish Arms there would be the fitting finale for my story.

In this village the ancient parish church and inn look over to each other to make the most pleasing of companions. a stone coffin was once found in the churchyard. It was said to have contained the body of one of the slaughtered kings from the battle. In the ancient 'Hundred of Amounderness' too, there is **Elston** village, the name having come down from Athelstan, the monarch here.

The beautiful stained glass windows in The Cavendish Arms, Brindle, depict scenes connected with the Battle of Brunanburg between Saxons and Vikings in AD937. The events were to change the course of our island's history.

Many of our old village inns are noted for preserving interesting relics of the past. The Cavendish Arms has a wonderful set of stained glass windows forming the lighting of the public and saloon bars. They depict battle scenes of the Viking-Saxon skirmish on the Ribble banks from that historic date. A particularly good one shows Athelstan being given a new sword to replace one he had broken during the fighting. Anluf the Dane is there, the Viking warriors, the English, and a corner panel bears the date of the epic event AD 937. Best of all, is a window showing the 'treasure' being buried above the river banks before the inglorious retreat.

There was a fair sprinkling of customers in both bars as I entered and my shorts-clad legs came in for a good share of humour and banter. The landlord readily granted my request to take photographs of the windows which in this lovely day of sunshine, just glowed with colour.

I had an interested audience as I carefully moved plants, bowls of flowers, oil lamps and brasses, to focus the camera for my pictures. There was a cheer when I finally moved everything back into place without damage, then to sit and enjoy my glass.

This had been a little run with a purpose in mind in reliving for me a little chapter of history, especially in my native Lancashire. Such days I regard as the very essence of the good cycle touring life I lead — personal magic moments bringing delight and contentment.

Most readers will probably have never heard of Brunanburg or AD 937 and historians over the years have disagreed where the battle was fought. To me though it was here, in Lancashire and on those plains sweeping to the Ribble. The 'treasure' and the Cuerdale Hoard stone are vivid but silent memories to ponder on.

If you are around this way, why not follow my wheels to browse down the memories of Anluf the Dane and Athelstan the first ruler of England.

7
Following the Way of Kilvert

". . . But some day will come the last illness from which there will be no convalescence and after which there will be no more sights and sounds of the earthly spring, the singing of the birds, the opening of the fruit blossoms, the budding dawn of green leaves, and the blowing of the March daffodils. May I then be prepared to enter into the everlasting Spring and to walk among the birds and flowers of Paradise".

LITTLE did the writer of these beautiful lines that speak so eloquently of the simple sights and sounds of nature and the countryside he loved, know that his premonition would be fulfilled so shortly afterwards on 23rd September, 1879, when he was only 38-years-old.

I knew the words so well, indeed I had committed them to memory and was reading them again from a diary in an old country churchyard facing his grave.

The place was **Bredwardine-on-Wye** in Herefordshire and the man whose story I was seeking was the Rev. Robert Francis Kilvert, who was vicar there between 1877-1879. Two years had passed by since I had first learned about Kilvert. The beautiful stories were enshrined in the pages of a wonderful diary he kept for nine years between 1870 and 1879. In it he had faithfully recorded a vivid and colourful picture of the countryside, its people, and the events of the time as they were happening. In addition to his own personal life's troubles and experiences, his gifted pen has left us with a rich literary inheritance of yesterday.

Much of the diary has its setting in Clyro in Radnorshire where Kilvert was curate between 1865 and 1872, and at Langley Burrell in Wiltshire, where again he was curate to his father between 1872 and 1876. After he had a short spell at St. Harmon's in Radnorshire, he became vicar of Bredwardine.

So deeply engrossed was I as the stories unfolded in the pages of his diary, that I was determined to follow some of the ways he described so long ago. That is why I had come with the bike to Bredwardine, the book of the diary in the saddlebag, ready to be opened and read many times during my ride.

Unhappily, circumstances had meant that my introduction to Kilvert was being made at the end of his short life and at the end of the year for me. For it was a dull, wintry and mist-enshrouded December day. To be precise, the 23rd December. The previous evening I had been well received and served at an excellent C.T.C. appointment in Hereford and had come with the Brecon-Hay highway to the valley of the Wye.

Though tempted several times to turn towards the river and cross it by elusive lanes dipping down to it, Bredwardine was so firmly fixed in my mind that I waited until I came to Staunton-on-Wye before turning aside. For I wanted the thrill of crossing Bredwardine bridge which Kilvert mentioned so many times. Besides, I should see his former vicarage and the church peeping through the trees nearby.

The Wye was so sullen-looking on this pre-Christmas day, its waters slipping so sulkily and silently by. Already I was experiencing a thrill of pleasure as I pedalled slowly over the bridge, took a left turning up a short lane and there it was, Bredwardine Church, so appealing in its setting.

This old church with its mellowed fabric, tower and old tombstones tangled with creeper and ivy and leaning at odd angles told of the fusion between past and present. Facing me was a gnarled old yew tree. Beneath it a memorial seat to Kilvert. Leaving the bike by the church gate, I walked the pathway to the entrance.

I was pleased to find it open. It was good to sit in a pew and read about its history. I learned that the chancel of early Norman work had been rebuilt in the 15th century after it had been destroyed by soldiers of Owen Glyndower in 1406. I was also fascinated by the two effigies of sleeping knights in the chancel, one of them in alabaster being Sir Robert Vaughan, killed at Agincourt; the other being a member of the noted Baskerville family, a name which was to occur several times during the day.

I could not resist walking up the steps of the pulpit to stand where Kilvert had often stood preaching his sermons to the village congrega-

The grave of 'Little Davie', in Bredwardine churchyard. He was buried on Christmas Day, 1878. The Cross was restored by The Kilvert Society in 1952.

tion. Turning the diary to Christmas Day 1878, I read the sad account of the death of 'Little' David Davies, a small boy eight years old, who had died two days previously. Kilvert told of the sad Christmas scene in the churchyard in deep snow.

Little Davie's grave and Kilvert's are close to each other on the north side of the churchyard. Later looking at them both, I realised that by amazing coincidence I was here on the Christmastime anniversary of Little Davie's death.

There were many other things to interest me in this old churchyard and was pleased to find and examine strange carvings over the 'Devil's Door' which Kilvert had shown to his father on one of his visits.

It was only a short distance to the village and facing the Red Lion Inn I sat astride the bike looking at my Ordnance map, tracing with my finger the way I should be taking on a circuitous route over Bredwardine Hill and back to the Red Lion in the village. The way I was choosing was a Kilvert way, for the good vicar would often walk this circuit, visiting the cottages and homes of his scattered congregation. At the hamlet of Crafta Webb was a house where he held a weekly service 'for the folk on the hill'.

I found the turning with ease. A signposted lane to Dorstone Hill made me realise that it was to be a steady push with the bike. As I climbed I wished the day could have been better, then I should have been rewarded with sweeping views of the Wye landscape from the many vantage points. Even so in the greyness of the morning I was looking at cottages and farmsteads which I knew would be little changed from the day and age Kilvert walked this way.

Suddenly looking down the side of a farm building, I saw the massive head of a buffalo staring at me with angry glassy eyes. At first I could not believe it but there was no mistake about it, it certainly was a buffalo head with great drooping ears and long curving horns. Entirely out-of-place in this Herefordshire lane even though the cycling tourist is always ready for the unexpected.

I had stopped to enjoy a cup of tea from the flask and munch a Christmas mincepie, and with the map open saw the words 'Arthur's Stone' so depicted, and realised that the next lane turning would take me there and better still, Kilvert knew this stone and had mentioned it in the diary. How I like

The Devil's Door Bredwardine Church.

those words depicted in old English letters on the Ordnance maps, offering a shadowy pattern of a link with an ancient or pre-historic past.

I had not expected finding such a perfect specimen of Neolithic tomb up here and eagerly examined it from every angle. The great uprights and capstone were still in position. What I was looking at was almost 4,000 years old. Originally it would have been covered by a mound of earth. Why it should have been called 'Arthur's Stone' I do not know, for it is certainly a long way off the knightly haunts of Camelot!

The lane had now levelled off and I knew I should have some thrilling descents to come very shortly as I approached the first beginning of Crafta Webb. Disaster almost struck whilst passing a farmyard, for I was suddenly attacked by two dogs barking and snapping at my heels and when I felt a tug on my stockings the cycle pump had to be brought into play. One of the dogs quickly retired yelping with a very much bruised nose. I wonder if Kilvert ever had to run the gauntlet of countryside dogs?

It was with caution that I took the first of the descents, for I was determined to find what remained of the old house where the good vicar

All that remains of the Crafta Webb House, where Kilvert once held a weekly service.

had held his weekly services. What a pitiful scene it was when I did indeed find it.

A few tumbled stones and a tottering chimney stack stood above the tangled hedgerow of the lane to my left. To get to it presented a problem, I would have to fight my way through a veritable jungle of blackberry fronds and branches. Twice my bob-cap was whisked off and once I became fairly stuck and enmeshed in it all. Perseverance was the key. I resorted to hands and knees and eventually stood by the ruined house to examine old timbers, peer up the chimney and look at what had been the old fireside oven.

It was an eerie experience to be there in the wintry gloom with spangled dew everywhere. did not these tumbled walls and ruined fireplace still hold the echoes of the good vicar's voice and the 'folk on the hill' also assembled here? Then opening the diary of his account to read of that severe winter of 1878-1879 when the Wye was frozen at Bredwardine Bridge and great ice floes were grinding and pushing the arches of the bridge made me shudder at the thought. In my mind's eye I could see people coming up the hill on all fours. To cross the Red Lion Square in the village one village lady had crawled on her hands and knees. Kilvert himself had come to give his service in a blinding snowstorm, carrying his lantern to light his way, on New Year's Day 1879. No doubt he could have had the warmth and solace of his vicarage fireside but never would he have missed this cottage meeting for the scattered people of the hill. I was seeing it all on the actual spot and through the pages of the diary.

Picking thorns and tangles from my stockings, trousers and jacket, and dabbing at a nasty scratch on my face, I placed the book back in the saddlebag, then it was down, down, and down back to Bredwardine —

a hair-raising descent with some 'one-in- fours' with both brakes hard on.

My turning to nearby **Hay-on-Wye** was there at the Red Lion in Bredwardine village. Even in the gloom I could admire high tree-topped slopes on my left and here and there I could see the river confined within grassy banks.

Hay-on-Wye was in festive mood with shoppers thronging the streets. A fish-and-chip scent assailed my nostrils and I 'nosed' it out to enjoy them with a steaming pot of tea, peas and bread and butter. Then it was a sweep out of town there to cross the Wye and pedal the short mile to **Clyro** village.

A little alarmed at first on seeing new houses in the village. I had no need to worry, for at the top-end of the village there was the Clyro of old with the graceful lines of the church commanding the picture. As expected, I found Clyro church much larger than Bredwardine, with a tall tower and extremely roomy interior.

Clyro Church, Radnorshire. Kilvert was Curate here for seven years. Most of his diary is centred around the district.

On this Christmas afternoon several ladies from the village were decorating the church for the season with holly, ferns, and Christmas tree branches and flowers. I was greeted with welcoming smiles and when they knew of my interest in Kilvert, was told and shown many things. I was shown a rare photograph of him hanging on an inner wall and a book of photographs — taken when the Kilvert Society was formed — was produced for my inspection. Also on the wall of the church I noticed a memorial plaque erected by the Society, recording the curacy of the diarist during his seven years there.

How beautiful and wonderful are these writings at Clyro, they are a pure joy to read. In them Kilvert through the magic of his pen, records the village scene to perfection. It is as if a colourful cavalcade of all the people he knew and wrote about can be seen walking from the pages down and along those pathways of the churchyard and through the avenue of yews to the delight of the Clyro countryside beyond.

He also tells of the emotion he felt when preaching his farewell sermon:-

> ". . . in the afternoon I preached my farewell sermon at Clyro . . . though the afternoon was so rainy there were a good many people in church. I don't know how I got through the service. It was the last time. My voice was broken and choked by sobs and tears, and I think the people in the church were affected too. Richard Brooks in the choir was crying like a child".

There were, however, to be return visits to the village, and times when he just simply had to pour out his innermost feelings and yearnings, especially on a day in 1874, when he wrote:

> ". . . I walked to Clyro by the old familiar fields and the Beacon stile and when I looked down upon the dear old village nestling round the church in the hollow at the dingle mouth and saw the fringes of the beautiful woods and the hanging orchards and the green slopes of Penllan and the white farms and cottages over the hills, a thousand sweet and sad memories came over me, and all my heart rose up within me and went out in love towards the beloved place and people among whom I lived so long and so happily".

At the churchyard gate where I had parked the bike, I picked up a sprig of holly which had been dropped by the ladies on their way to the church. I tucked it beneath the cape straps as a Christmas garland, then wheeled the bike by the churchyard wall to the Baskerville Arms. Facing me there was 'Ashbrook' where Kilvert lodged during his curacy at Clyro. I had seen monuments to the Baskerville both within and outside the church as well as the knight at Bredwardine. Did, perhaps the author of the thrilling story 'Hound of the Baskervilles' adopt his plot from this area?

Time had passed all so quickly. Already the deepening dusk of the short wintry day was cloaking the church tower as I pedalled an almost deserted road above the Wye. It was so good to cycle in the soft quietness of this winter's night, the dynamo giving a satisfying whirl and the lampbeam lighting the way ahead.

A dreamy-like nostalgia was forming. I would have given so much to have known Kilvert in his time and age, which he had so vividly captured in his diary. He never knew of the bicycle, for his were the days of dog-carts, horses, carriages, candles and lanterns.

I feel sure, however, he had been with me in spirit, smiling at my having followed some of his ways.

8

The Melody of Pendle

"JESUS shall reign where'er the sun,
Doth his successive journeys run,
His Kingdom stretch from shore to shore,
Till moons shall wax, and wane no more."

I WOULD say, without hesitation, that you will readily recognise these words as being the first verse of one of the world's most beautiful hymns. No doubt you sang it during your childhood, or during your youth. If you are of mature years you will know it well.

Now, can I ask you to read the verse again and as you do so, hum or sing the words — either to yourself or better still, sing it aloud. The reason I ask is because there are two popular tunes to the hymn; a very old one called 'Gallilee' and a more modern one called 'Rimington'. Both are lovely, but though I do not know much about the tune of 'Gallilee', should you have chosen it, I can tell you much about the tune of 'Rimington' — 'The Melody of Pendle' — and the memory of the man who composed it.

Of the thousands throughout the world who know the tune by its name, I am sure few realise its dedication to the little village of the same name that nestles so well by the flanks of Pendle Hill, and blends perfectly into the scene. I go there often when on my Pendle wanders.

If you chose 'Rimington' and the echo of the tune is still with you, why not join me along these Pendle lanes and all in good time I will lead you to Rimington. There I shall unfold for you the colourful and fascinating story of it all.

Over breakfast, I had listened to the radio weather man, who had not been optimistic about the day, promising showers (some heavy at times), but with some "bright periods". Such reports do not worry me I was in fine fettle as I quickly put the 20 miles behind me from my Lancashire home-town to **Whalley**, on the threshold of the **Ribble Valley**.

52

The hymn tune 'Rimington' was made into a postcard (above). Soon after it was printed over two million were sold.

I always like to stop for coffee in Whalley with a bun or a cake to go with it. Seated with the map unfolded, I planned the next part of my ride to the Craven uplands. With ample time to spare told myself: "Aye, this is a morning for a detour through the Pendle lanes, through **Worston, Downham** and **Rimington**, and then onwards to **Gisburn** in time for lunch".

I had learned of a 'memorial plaque' to the composer of 'Rimington' placed in position there and I wanted to photograph it.

Up to a few years ago, my introduction to the Pendle lanes had always been made at Barrow village on the outskirts of Clitheroe, where a sharp right turn provided enchanting views of the hill all the way to Worston. The building of the Whalley and Clitheroe Bypass unhappily severed the lanes, yet the Barrow entrance still remains a 'No Through Road', guarded by a stout padlocked gate. Happily, a wicker gate by its side gives entrance to the walker and cyclist and the lovely miles we knew of yore have been preserved.

I wheeled the bike through and immediately relished the lovely feeling of peace and solitude. A lane left behind from 'progress', with hawthorn tangles at the verges, flanking fields and meadows and with cows and sheep grazing. In the pleasantry of the morning I loved it all. At **Standen**, the lane dips down to a little dingle and here for a few moments I was content to stand on the bridge looking down to the fast-flowing brook. I would like to think there are other cyclists like myself, who like to indulge in looking over bridges, sharing the interest in nature, the pattern of trees, the rich scents of moist earth and the chatter of a woodland brook; simple pleasures maybe, but sheer delight and joy.

All too soon the lane ended at its entrance by the A59 highway. Just before reaching there, I looked over to **Pendle** which was dominating the scene and clear-cut against the sky. I only tolerated the busy highway for a short distance, crossing it to where the 'lost lane' continued on the far side. In a twinkling, I was pedalling into **Worston village**.

I like the way old Worston retains its ancient character and charm. The pleasing stone cottages fronted by cobbles, a dimpling stream and the old Calf's Head Inn. The inn faces the foot of an extremely steep hill and I remember in my younger days being told the story of how the landlord always kept his front door open so that the old riders of 'penny-farthings' speeding too fast down the hill, could ride through the door and along the inn passage to the yard outside. I was told, too, that the village blacksmith did a roaring trade straightening out wheels.

From Worston to Downham is but a mile or so but the lanes there are spiced with rascality. They dip and climb, twist and turn and you really do have to be on the alert with the brakes and gears. Pendle is continually

Beautiful Downham Village.

in view and when it is all over, Downham village is waiting there to display its manifold attractions.

The story book of countryside England is covered with many chapters portraying the age-old attractions of the village scene. Each and every county offers its own particular contribution to the traditional village picture of yesterday. Without doubt Downham has long been the choice of Lancashire.

First, at the foot of the steep hill that climbs through the village, is the dainty bridge over the stream. Always each time I go, there seems to be an increase in the mallard population waiting for thrown tit-bits. The bridge and stream take the eye on to the hoary old manor house and then, by trim cottages, to the hilltop where the village church sits looking down in benign manner.

At the top of hill there is a pocket-handkerchief green, graced by the remains of stone stocks and shaded by a gnarled old sycamore. That backward glance down and above the village is perfection, with Pendle forming the backcloth. Look carefully around and you will not see any discordant or ugly overhead wires or cables to mar the scene, for everything was placed underground.

I had a few minutes on the convenient seat by the stocks and sycamore and was joined by two cycling fathers, out with their respective sons on new bicycles; all of them enjoying this, their first visit to Downham.

As I left Pendle had sun shadows on his brow. I detected too, a few menacing clouds intruding over the white and blue. It was time for 'elevenses' and I like to choose my spots, if possible, in hidden haunts of quietude. What better than to turn beyond Downham church to take the lane to Rimington, stopping to open a gate before a bridge skirting a woodland verge. Then to pass beneath a railway bridge that dipped me down to Swanside Beck — a tributary of the Ribble that formerly marked the boundary between Lancashire and Yorkshire.

So lovely is this beck. Its beauty is enhanced by the delightful packhorse bridge of extreme ancient vintage and retaining its memory of the heydey of its use. I chose the base of a beech tree to spread the cape, to open the flask and enjoy the coffee in the silence and thrilled to see a squirrel scampering a few feet away, along a wall-top before disappearing into the trees.

I retraced my way to Downham Bridge and as I pedalled the lane towards Rimington, Pendle was very much in the picture, although a sky battle was taking place above his summit with threatening storm clouds ousting the blue. A few turns of the pedals now and I was entering

Rimington, greeting it like an old friend. Most of the houses of the village have Pendle as their main view and I noticed for the first time that one facing row of houses was called 'Pendle Terrace'.

Rimington does not claim any special fame in the Pendle story. I am sure that on Christmas Day, 1862, when Francis Duckworth was born there, the event did not arouse any special excitement. He was still a young boy when the family moved to nearby Stopper Lane, where next door to the Wesleyan Chapel, they kept the village shop.

The storm clouds were winning and the first drops of rain were falling as I turned sharp right for the short ride to Stopper Lane where I should once again be able to recapture the next chapter of the story of 'The Hymn of Pendle'.

Stopper Lane was deserted and I leaned the bike by the wall of the Post Office, which is still the village shop as the Duckworth family knew it. In those mid-Victorian days, the hymns of England were sung with a greater fervency than they are today. They were sung with gusto at the tiny village schools by the children and by the farm labourers in the fields. Who cannot fail to be enchanted by the memory pictures of cottage scenes when the day's work was done; when in the mellow glow from oil lamps and around the fireside there would be reading from the scriptures and families would join in the singing of favourite hymns.

The name of the Rev. Isaac Watts stands out as one of the masters of English hymn-writing, and 'Jesus shall reign . . . ' was one of his finest, which he penned in 1719.

One day in this village shop at Stopper Lane, the uncle of young Francis Duckworth, who was a great admirer of the old hymn, remarked during a discussion with one of his customers: ". . . Jesus shall reign where'er the sun", and followed his words with: "Where'er the sun. . . Ah — Watts had the conception; he said more in one line than your modern hymn writers say in a whole hymn".

The words had, unknowingly, created a deep impression on Francis, who had been listening. He was always to remember them. In later years he became a gifted musician and composer — his favourite instrument being the organ. Thirty years, however, were to pass before he was to compose his own tune to Watts' hymn. Remembering the scene of his boyhood days in the village shop, he named it 'Rimington', dedicating it to the village where he had been born.

More hymn tunes were to come from his pen but 'Rimington' was to be his crowning glory. Today, it is known world-wide and choirs up to 40,000 strong have sung the words and his hymn tune to them. A wonderful occasion was the singing of it by a company of soldiers on Mount Calvary.

The Wesleyan Chapel is now but a memory, a trim dwelling having been made from it, but I shall always treasure the memory of visiting it, when I first learned the story of 'Rimington'. I peeped inside and walked to the organ there that Francis knew so well. Somehow I just had to sit down and play the first few bars of the hymn. A

On the gravestone of Francis Duckworth in Gisburn Church Yard is inscribed the first line and tune of 'Jesus shall reign where'er the sun'.

pity the chapel had to go, but then we live in an age when many of our countryside churches and chapels are disappearing.

Nevertheless I was pleased to see the memorial plaque in position and though the rain was falling and I had to wriggle into my cape, I sheltered my camera and focused on the words:-

"FRANCIS DUCKWORTH. Composer of the Hymn tune RIMING-TON, spent his childhood at the adjoining shop, and worshipped in this building which was formerly THE METHODIST CHAPEL".

Had the village shop been open, I would certainly have entered for they sold ice-cream. In the little window I could see glass jars of old favourite sweets — pear drops, marzipan cakes, winter mixture and mouth-watering black humbugs.

A little side lane took me out of Stopper Lane to **Martin Top** and towards the Gisburn road. Hurrah, the rain was stopping, and Pendle was coming out again from the grey and black clouds. Sky spaces were soon opening and blue brought the sunshine to sparkle on the wet gleaming fields. A lovely transformation was to follow above the Pendle scene and when I topped a small hill, I could look down above a mosaic of green to the distant and far-reaching view of the Craven highlands. Out there, too, were the 'big three' — **Whernside, Ingleborough,** and **Penyghtne** — and I was experiencing the lovely feeling that I would be seeing them at close quarters later during the day.

The hoary old tower of Gisburn church made an inspiring and tranquil picture in the afternoon sunshine and I therefore decided to make one last pilgrimage as it were, to look at the grave of Francis Duckworth, which lies at the rear of the church. In addition to the epitaph, there is engraved into the stone the first line of the hymn and the music of 'Rimington'. To me, it is a beautiful contribution to the heritage of Pendle and to a memory so refreshing to those of us who know and love its ways.

9

'Overland' to the Cape

". . . Hardy walkers (even cyclists of exceptional determination) can follow the uninhabited coast up to Cape Wrath".

THAT was it — the caption to the picture of Sandwood Bay that appeared in a past issue of *Cycling* some years ago. I had looked up the issue especially to refresh my memory and smiled in contentment as I looked at the picture. The memory of it all came flooding back to me.

Had the picture been taken on a morning two weeks later, there would have been two sets of cycle tracks across that lovely unblemished sandy expanse. From atop of the cliff tops seen in the picture, the rear of two cyclists of "exceptional determination" would also have been seen. They were "setting off" on their hard way 'Overland' to the Cape.

To tell you that we 'did it', would perhaps not convey much to you. But let me tell you how we did it and ask you to share with us the tears, sweat, and toil that it entailed. Perhaps, you may then be tempted, before the bones begin to creak and old man rheumatism stabs his fingers into your joints, to follow our ways.

'Overland' to the Cape had always been one of my ambitions. Here I was, almost ten years to the day back in Scotland, with my good cycling companion Steve and relishing every minute of the wealth of natural beauty of the north-west highlands. We had had our fair share of rain, grey misty days and wet camps. Then came the day when the highlands atoned for such behaviour and in the kindliness of that day, the sun was burnishing the skies and as our wheels took us further and further north-westwards, thrilled to the spectacular grandeur of it all.

Lovely it was to recapture the coastal scenes. Memories of little Scourie, the lochans fringing the headland dip to Laxford Bridge, Eddrachillis and Rhiconish, where we had seen the signpost to Durness. Ah, but that was not for us. That was the 'easy' way to **Cape Wrath**.

Our way was to swing sharp left, both of us now on new territory, as we rode the high way above **Loch Inchard.**

The tops were clear cut against the early evening sky. A beautiful mellow light was gilding the loch, sparkling the surface in dancing light. We pedalled lazily, many times stopping with the cameras in play. It was so nice to receive an arm-raised greeting from a most amused tractor-driving farmer pulling a load of peat.

We had another stop at **Kinlochbervie** to gaze down at the picture of the fishing boats anchored close together, and here too, we had a few moments of amusement. A village man noting our bikes loaded with camping equipment, informed us we were cycling towards a "dead-end" and that "there was no good camping up there".

We did not enlighten him about our ultimate destination; Steve remarked: "Oh, we'll find somewhere". Then it was on again. The immediate northward scene appearing rather bleak and barren, giving us the first taste of what was in store.

Now and then, looking southwards, we could see the sea sparkling in reflected sunshine and here and there exciting tiny byways branching aside to the shores, which we would have liked to have explored had time permitted. Beyond the handful of dwellings was **Blairmore,** and there was the sign (just a simple wooden board) we had been waiting for. It pointed through a gate to **Sandwood Loch** (No Dogs Allowed). It was there we began the trail, eager for the wild surprises and challenges on the waiting vast uninhabited wilderness of the Parbh that lay so far before us. Both of us were agreeably surprised at the rough but wide track, which with care we could ride. We quickly passed the small Loch Aisir on our right, and almost within minutes were skirting the shores of the larger Loch na Gainimh, appreciating the bright splash of colour it made to the otherwise austere scene.

Save for the whispers of the evening breeze and the wild call of the dipping seabirds, there was an air of silence everywhere.

The track was well 'cairned' and unmistakable, leading us by a few more small lochs. Then at a point where we began to descend we could see the conspicuous deep high valley cutting across the scene, and knew that it could only be **Strath Shinary,** whose many streams, burns and feeders, terminate in Sandwood Loch, and its outlet via the bay of the same name, to the sea.

Sure enough, as we began to descend towards the Strath, the loch came into view. Immediately I was enchanted with what I was seeing. There and then I would have descended to it, but Steve gently reminded me there were more urgent things to do, for it was almost 9 p.m. and we had still to find a place to camp.

We investigated a lonely bothy some distance away, but the litter it contained together with the lingering unripe scents, decided us to camp instead. Though open to the strong wind now blowing from the bay, a ruined sheep fold on top of a green turfed hill was the obvious choice. With one accord, the bikes were wheeled and twisted inside to the centre. Then of all things, we began to play football! The 'footballs' were the heaps of sheep droppings that littered the turf. Steve indulged in some masterly manoeuvres, kicking for 'goal' towards the entrance.

With gloves on we attacked the thistles and nettles to clear a space for the two lightweight tents. Snug and comfortable and sitting at the tent doors, we prepared our late evening meal. The approaching dusk seemingly reluctant to steal away the joys and glory of the summer evening. Somehow, I sensed the night hours would come all serene.

They did just that. At six a.m. we were up, washing, cooking and packing. Happy to greet the dazzling splendour of the warming sun; it was the first day of July. By 7.45 a.m. we were away allowing plenty of time for what lay ahead.

Our green hill was a vast rabbit warren. They lolloped and scurried away as we began the descent to **Sandwood Bay**. We found the easiest way was down some sand dunes to the shore and this is where I shall remind my readers of the two sets of wheel tracks across the unblemished shores of the bay. We were exercising the utmost care because we had heard stories of lurking quicksands in the area, especially on the outlet flow from the loch to the sea.

I shall never forget the memory of Sandwood Bay on that high summer's morning. It far excelled everything I had read or heard about it. The pageantry of the ever restless sea was there to perfection. Huge breakers coming in, foaming blue and breaking dazzling white on the shores. High unyielding cliffs gloriously encircled the bay. Lashed by the sea, spray leapt skywards in confusion. Also out there, standing sentinel apart from the cliffs, was a huge 'stack' rock, with a thousand milling and screaming gulls around and about it.

At this stage too, dear reader, I shall reveal that Sandwood is one of the very few places where a 'mermaid' can be seen. I am told she is a beautiful creature with all the curves in the right places, and that she will lure you on to a secret lair beneath the waves. I did not see her but there is the strange story of Sandy Gunn, a shepherd. On the record is his "authenticated account" of the incident.

Sandy had missed one of his sheep, which had strayed to the headlands to the shore and promptly he sent his dog to round it up. He heard the dog whimpering and when he went to investigate, there she was at the shore's edge, presenting to him a 'come-hither' smile. Very wisely Sandy promptly retreated in double quick time, thoroughly scared. I am told that Sandy was not the same man after his 'meeting' and most certainly never indulged in taking a 'wee dram' during his shepherding duties.

We had expected having to paddle across the shallows of Sandwood Loch. How thankful we were to see the flimsy footbridge there, which we crossed safely. Certainly it saved us from the dangers of quicksands. The next obstacle was an awkward wire fence. The two of us took each bike in turn, sharing the front and rear wheels, we lifted them over with ease without having to unload. High rocks followed and we tackled them by choosing our steps with care. Panting with exertion we reached higher and level ground.

Now the one-inch Ordnance map was in use. We made a careful study and reconnaissance of it at Sandwood and resolved to keep close to the coast. There would have to be several detours to tackle a few awkward

How thankful we were to see this flimsy footbridge. It certainly saved us from the dangers of quicksand. In the background Sandwood Bay.

The no mans land of the Parhb.

hills by passing between them but we did not expect too much difficulty from the two rivers, the map indicated.

We passed a small lochan and when we came to the first river, the Chailleach, we knew we were on course. Making our way up rising terrain to a depression between two distant hills called Cnoc a'Gheadha and Bealach Cnoc na h-Uidhe (how these ancient names fascinate me).

Savage and severe, yet appealing in its solitude is this wilderness of the Parbh — a veritable no-man's-land, shunned by sensible people. There are no distinct paths, ways, or tracks over it, and I have no hesitation in saying it should never be attempted alone. There are many hazards and difficulties to be encountered. In inclement weather or sea mist, it could be a death trap. A sudden innocent fall or tumble resulting in a wrenched or sprained ankle or broken leg could mean disaster for the 'loner'. Days or weeks could pass by without a person going there. Moreover there are innocent-looking patches of green that hide deep unsavoury bogs.

We made very slow but steady progress, taking our time with many stops for breathers, and we were almost level with Loch a 'Gheodha Ruaidh before we realised it was there. This was another of our objective points achieved. We celebrated with another ten minutes or so of rest, laughing and chatting away.

Next followed a comparatively flat portion, with dense cotton grass in evidence. Gradually we were slanting down to the second river — this time a fast flowing one, that was tumbling into a dark rocky strewn ravine. Looking along its length we could see the coast for the first time since Sandwood. Again there was a fence to be crossed, repeating our 'two to a bike' lift. We found we had to walk some distance up river to find a suitable place to ford it. This was the Keisgaig River, coming from the unseen loch of the same name tucked away in a fold of the Parbh.

There was to follow now the toughest part of the crossing. Up on the horizon were the twin hills of Sithean na h-lolaireich and Cnoc a' Ghiubhais. A red granite outcrop showing clear and between them a knoll-like depression which we should have to cross.

With our eyes continually riveted on that red splash and the depression, we began the long push, the haul and the heave. There were rocks and boulders, tangled heather tussocks and vegetation and innumerable weather and waterworn channels to surmount and pass over. Our many rests and stops gradually dwindled from 100 yards or so, to 20 yards or even less, and it was a good moment when finally we achieved it, only to flop down with relief. Two juicy oranges refreshed us.

From our high vantage point there it was, a long way ahead, the twisting and winding road cutting its way across the Parbh to vanish behind the headland to **Cape Wrath**. A few minutes later we were to see a slow moving white dot; it was the mini-bus on its way to the lighthouse with its sight-seeing passengers.

There was no holding us now. Down and down we plunged, taking the many peat runnels in our stride and keeping the heavily-laden bikes in check. Until at long last we 'surfaced' a little beyond the two-mile post to the Cape. It had taken five-and-a- quarter hours from Sandwood. It was so strange at first to feel a solid surface beneath the wheels and we soon made short work of the remaining ride to the lighthouse.

Dramatic and stimulating was the experience of walking the massive headland of the Cape, with a sense of achievement at standing on the north-westerly tip of Scotland. The wind was screaming defiance in unison with the thronging gulls and gannets. Looking back the way we had come, there it was the little match-stick size stack rock of Sandwood at the foot of dark cliffs.

In the water bottle was a pint of best Keisgaig river water, and we had to huddle behind the white bollard gate stone of the lighthouse entrance to shield the stove from the wind. The coffee made at Cape Wrath tasted like nectar and was appreciated more than any celebration bottle of champagne.

This 11 miles long road from Keoldale Durness to Cape Wrath was constructed to serve the lighthouse and links with the ferry over the Kyle of Durness. In addition to its lighthouse duties, the mini-bus (the only vehicle) conveys small parties of visitors to the Cape. During slack periods, cyclists can take advantage of the small ferry boat, with the 22 miles return trip to the Cape being a unique experience.

Our ride back towards Durness was taken in a slow leisurely manner. The sun was shining, the day was good and we were still basking in the glow of our achievement. We even made a detour to see the mighty cliffs of Clo Mor which are over 800 feet high — the highest on the mainland. It was early evening when we presented ourselves at the cottage of the ferryman at **Daill**.

Now the ferryman keeps a close tally on all the visitors he brings over. He knows just how many cyclists there should be. After all it would never do to 'miss someone out' and have them roaming the Parbh or being 'marooned' as it were.

He looked at us, first with amazement, then with obvious amusement. I could sense him thinking'. There should be no cyclists on this side of the water . . . at least I have not brought any over today. He said: "Have you come from Sandwood?" I told him we had and both uf us were waiting for the 'dreaded' answer which could very well have been: "Well jolly well go back that way!"

But no, the ferryman is a kindly fellow with a twinkle in his eye and two lovely children and a good wife to make his days happy. He pointed to a sandbank which the tide would have to cover, before he could ferry us over. I told him that most probably we should be sleeping in the sunshine and please would he waken us up when he was ready.

The bikes were eventually loaded into the small boat and the whole family came along as well. The two girls laughing as we had to doff our shoes and socks, to wade by the boat and to shoulder the bikes to dry land. So ended our "Overland to the Cape" adventure but there was to be a most amusing climax to it all.

Some years ago, and it is still in existence, the Cape Wrath Fellowship was formed for cyclists, who have:

Ridden a bicycle from Keoldale
Ferry Durness, to Cape Wrath
Lighthouse, at the north-western
extremity of the Scottish mainland

Steve and I, had, walked and ridden a bicycle **from** Cape Wrath Lighthouse **to** Keoldale Ferry Durness.

Please, oh please, I wrote to the then Secretary of the Fellowship, accept us as elected members, even though we have not strictly observed the entry conditions. Two weeks later, we received the coveted Certificate of Membership and 'natty' blazer badges to wear.

POSTCRIPT:

Some years later I had the pleasure of leading a small party of cycling 'veterans' to the Cape along the lighthouse road, and on a superb day of sunshine, they were spellbound with it all. I joined them in their enthusiasm on reaching the Cape though I could not resist looking longingly back in the direction of Sandwood.

10

Retreat from the 'High Street'

TAKE the Saturday scene in the high streets of any of our large town or cities and what do you find? Most certainly there will be a milling and pushing shopping crowd. Prams, pushchairs, shopping bags and baskets and barking dogs on leads to hamper progress will all be found. There will be motor cars creeping and crawling along with a veritable cacophony of sounding horns to add to the noise of it all.

Now what if the unfortunate cyclist in his wanderings should happen to come on such a scene? My advice to him would be to make a hasty retreat to less frequented ways. But the sensible cyclist always avoids the high street at all costs!

But wait — the story I shall unfold to you is of an entirely deserted high street. Spectacular, fascinating and thrilling, upon which we cycled, but from which we had to beat the hastiest of retreats!

Perhaps one or two of you may have already guessed where my 'high street' is. If not, it is that hair-raising Roman road of the same name that strides well-known 'tops' in Lakeland and which for well nigh on 2,000 years has retained their memory.

At an age when most of the Lakeland tracks and passes had fallen to my wheels 'high street' still remains a challenge. Often when in the area, I would look with eyes of longing to the lofty heights where I knew the 'street' lay and I knew I should never be content until I had traversed its length from Eamont to Ambleside.

Several times too, I had spoken of the venture to my good friends Arthur and John. With their 'terrier noses' for adventure, were equally 'raring to go'. That is why on an early spring weekend, we met on Friday evening at the homely little **Thirlmere Youth Hostel**, with the 'venture' definitely on!

The week-end was true to our usual pattern, the Friday after-work rush, the meeting at the appointed hostel, the pre-supper chores, and then, ah that lovely feeling of being able to relax over a well-filled teapot, with the map spread out on the table. How I relish this satisfying feeling of a good week-end before me, in good cycling company, with the awaited joys of the morrow. Such pleasures, fostered from my younger days, are, in my veteran years cherished so much more. My crowded cycling life has been good to me and yet there is so much more I want to see and do in my remaining wheeling years.

As to our plans, we would go back to Dunmail along the lake shores, and then we would take the wild pass over Grisedale flanking the Dollywaggon and Helvellyn, and then after our ride along Ullswater, we would cross the River Eamont, to seek our introduction to the 'high street'.

Was it not Burns who said:

The best laid schemes o'mice and men...Gang aft a-gley.

We stepped out of the hostel door next morning to see a Lakeland of high spring triumph. Ahead beyond the Vale of St. John's, were Skiddaw and Saddlebag, topped and mantled with snow, flaunted their beauty against a rich blue cloudless sky. Itchy fingers were on the cameras and our well laid plans had been blown sky high in a twinkling. The spring splendour and harmony of the two mountains could not be resisted. We just had to see them from a closer vantage point.

We therefore cycled up the vale to Lowthwaite and Wanthwaite, there to swing aside on to a 'green' road we knew of old. This would take us by Mosedale Beck to **Dockray village**. By so doing, we should have the continually rewarding views of Skiddaw and Saddleback for most of the way.

Sparkling and clear was the morning, it was good to pass through a farmyard and then feel the turf beneath the wheels. Backward glances revealed not only the Vale of St. John's but the distant Vale of Keswick with a snowy white and clear-cut against the sky. There are those who say this green fell road approach to Ullswater is dull and uninteresting. Fie on them, I say. It is a jolly road, dipping and climbing a way of mischief. Long stretches are rideable and there definitely should be a stop at Mosedale Beck Bridge, where the beck romps down from its beginnings on Great Dodd.

We hit the tarmac a mile or so before Dockray and then it was a freewheel down to the village, and all with one accord to park the bikes by the side of the village inn for excellent morning coffee and home-made biscuits.

Bright sunlight filtered into the low beamed room and every garden in the village was displaying daffodils. A quick stop at nearby Matterdale church so appealing this morning with its old-fashioned gas lamp at jaunty angle by the tower, and again daffodils everywhere in full trumpet. Then we began to thread the maze of lanes between Great and Little Mell Fells.

Baldhow, Greenrow, Brownrigg and Birchclose — not forgetting Thackwaite and Southwaite. How about these for lovely old Lakeland names to roll from the tongue as fitting appetizers for the larger **Dacre village**, where we stopped to look through the church and gaze over the wall at the impressive Dacre Castle, now a residence of note?

Then it was a tumble down through more lanes to eventually reach the River Eamont with a tempting swinging footbridge to cross to meadows on the far side. The bridge bristled with 'Private' notices; an enquiry from the rosy apple-cheeked lady of the nearby Mill House brought a smile of welcome and permission to cross the meadows which would take us to the remote **hamlet of Barton** where, in a setting of solitude, we found the little church, and again the daffodils were so golden and prolific, contrasting with rich green lawns.

Hurrah, the jackets were off as we lazed in the warm sun by the church lych-gate. The stove was soon roaring away and two pints of tea went down very well with the sandwiches we made and the cake. Oh yes and the fruit. We look after ourselves very well, thank you!

For a full hour we lazed there after our meal soaking up the sunshine and occasionally glancing and pointing to the fells far ahead, where cunningly concealed was the approach to our 'Mecca', the 'high street'.

As we had been indulging in our lazy somnolence we had failed to notice a large black cloud. Was it an omen? Little did we know of the events that were to follow!

On the bikes again, we quickly reached and crossed the Pooley Bridge-Penrith highway, climbing steadily in the direction of the 'streets' beginnings at Celleron but to take a minor lane past Winder Hall. On opening a gate the fells were before us and within minutes we were on the 'street'.

What a tremendous task it must have been for the Roman master-builders to make this highway, which has its determined stride over this eastern mountain spur of the Lakes. Seeing it today, it is hard to realise that there would be a regular coming and going of soldiers, chariots and horse traffic. The street would be a vital link in their road system between Carlisle and the garrison at Ambleside. From the lofty heights, any would be invader could readily be spotted by the patrolling soldiers — though I suspect Roman soldiers would curse beneath their breath at being assigned to duty on the 'street'.

On their leaving the 'street', just like the rest of the Roman lines of communication, it fell into disuse. There are stories of the 'street' being used by robbers and highwaymen and also, surprisingly, as a favourite venue for the Lakeland men to take part in horse racing and various sports.

The sunshine we had so relished throughout the day had, alas, now gone. Dark hovering clouds served to remind us we were approaching a historic mystery. A herd of fell ponies that had been quietly grazing took off at our approach. What a dramatic picture they made in full gallop, manes and tails flying to the breeze. I had a glow of pleasure in seeing them so free and unfettered in these solitudes of the fells.

We were surprised to see direction signs at a crossroads and ahead was a conspicuous green-like depression denoting a beck, where we hoped there would be level ground for the tents. We were carrying lightweight camping equipment for what was to be our first camp of the year. Secretly, I was hoping for a dramatic dawn picture of the 'street' though I had not dared to tell the others, otherwise there might have been 'words' about my doubtful sanity.

The Ordnance map had warned us we would pass a 'Stone Circle'. How delighted we were to see such a perfect example with the stones ringed in the traditional pattern. I wonder what the Romans thought about this 'circle' and whether they were subject to superstitions at having it so near their 'street'. I feel sure they would have respected it by not plundering the stones.

Only yards past the 'circle' was the beck flowing down to a small ravine, on the lip of which was a turfy expanse simply asking for the erection of the tents. They were up in the proverbial 'jiffy' and so good it was to sit at the doors over our meal, looking over the beck to the 'circle', and up there on a curving hilltop were the fell ponies obviously curious at what we were doing here.

Over the last cup of coffee we watched scurrying clouds across a leaden sky, expecting any minute the threatened storm. It was not to be, however, and we were to have something definitely unexpected — the full fury of a Lakeland snow blizzard. At first the flakes came in a billowy dance, and then whipped by the wind, we were to be completely enveloped in a white swirling mass.

Each of us hurriedly closed the tent doors, and secured the flysheets, and I anchored the doors down with additional pegs to stand the onslaught.

It was a weird experience sitting there, listening to the roar and the noise of the driving snow on the flysheet. Soon I had to resort to banging on the sides of the tent with my hand as I realised that heavy drifting was taking place, and if the storm continued, the low tents could quite easily be covered completely, and we could perhaps have been in trouble. Shouts from 'next door' told me John and Arthur were doing the same thing.

Unzipping the fly-sheet, I risked a peep outside. The bikes, which had been lying on their sides below the beck bank, had completely disappeared. Three smooth mounds marked their resting places. The standing stones of the 'circle' looked so dark and sinister in the swirling mass, to seemingly mock us in ironic comment at having dared to choose this high place on the 'street' for the night.

For something like an hour the blizzard raged and it was almost dark before we were able to venture outside and view the scene. Up to eighteen inches of snow lay in drifts around the tents. What an amusing picture we were to make as we set about clearing the sides from snow using the cooking pans as shovels and scoops.

It was to be an extremely cold night, yet lying in the warmth of the sleeping bag, listening to the wind and the snow flurries driving against the tent was a satisfying experience.

Here was England and the unexpected in weather. Early spring, when everything should have been green and bursting on the fells was the thickest blanket of deep crisp snow.

The water bucket was frozen solid, so I had to resort to filling the pan with snow to make the tea . . . and it takes a lot of snow to make a pint! The three of us sat there over breakfast thrilling to the display from the frosty skies as the sun broke free from the clouds, flooding the fells in dazzling brightness. Even the standing stones in their white smocks, now looked so warm and friendly towards us

One thing was certain, our proposed venture along the 'street' would have to be cancelled. It would have been foolhardy to have attempted it with the bikes in the deep snow. One false step on lurking ice could perhaps have resulted in disaster.

Wintry camp on 'High Street' and our inglorious retreat.

Instead we 'de-iced' the tents, fighting a battle to compress them into their usual small compass to pack them away. We dug out the bikes and dusted them down, and then to our disappointment our inglorious retreat from the 'high street' had to be made.

We stopped at the signpost before taking now the high and wide path down to **Pooley Bridge** for a panorama of rare beauty was there deep down below. Ullswater lay placid in white enchantment, reflecting the snow shrouds of the surrounding fells and peaks, yet down there too were differing shades of green where the valleys and fields had escaped the fury of the storm.

Coffee in Pooley Bridge, and then with ample time before us we sought the bridleway along the eastern shores of the lake, stopping often and lazing the morning away, for there were lovely vistas everywhere.

'High street' had mockingly defeated us but we were determined to be back. We would wait for a summer week-end, and camp again on the sward by the 'circle'. We would begin too, where we had left off, and follow in the footsteps of the Romans. From their lofty ways we would look down with the bikes on the Lakeland glory below.

We did just that a few months later, on a golden day of summer when all Lakeland was singing in nature's high triumph and we too, were singing that rousing and wll known refrain:

"Life can be so sweet
On the sunny side of the 'Street'.

11

The Magnificent Views of the High Pyrenees

I HAVE been told that the most magnificent view in the whole of the High Pyrenees is to be seen from a spur of the mountains above the snow girdled lake of Brazato, reached by a 'camino mulas' from the Balneario de Panticosa in Spain.

It is something to haunt the vision for all time. A display of mountain majesty one only sees on a few occasions in a lifetime. Up there from the summit ridges of the Brazato one may look down to the mighty Pico de Vignemale bestriding the Franco-Spanish frontier — all 10,800 feet of her from top to toe displaying her glistening snowcaps and savage glaciers.

I realised and shall always know that I was cheated of this rare experience by a mere half mile and 600 feet of ascent. Yet the enduring memory of that day I climbed with the bike the 'camino mulas' (mule track) to **Lango Brazato** will be forever golden - a treasured highlight of my cycling life.

How we toiled and sweated that afternoon up the Valle do Tena, a hot sultry afternoon with the mountains ringing us round like dominating giants. There had been thunder rumbles and an occasional flash of lightning over the snow peaks.

At **Escarilla** we were only a few cycling miles from the French frontier but our way lay along the Garganta del Escalar up twisting switchbacks. I was perfectly happy with my 20-ish gear, sitting the saddle comfortably, my two younger companions performing devilish-like dances as they 'honked' their way on much higher gears.

Such was the severity of the climb, I was not surprised when a resounding crack denoted that one of the young ones had broken his chain. Granted, I welcomed the rest sitting on a wall with my legs dangling above the gorge as the chain was repaired.

We reached the **Balnearios** in early evening. Our first impression was one of the surprise at finding the collection of hotels and buildings at this high altitude of 5,000 feet, especially as the valley is a cul-de-sac.

Cyclists are a rarity there, judging by the interest and excitement we caused as we parked the bikes by the reception building. We were shown to sparsely-furnished rooms in an outbuilding and before supper had time for a walk round the spa. The focal point was the lake certainly in a superb setting with snow capped rocky peaks plummeting sheer to the water.

We walked until the dusk stole up the valley and standing on a bridge under which the icy river poured to the lake, we could feel, as it were, those frowning mountains above us. Tomorrow we would be at grips with them on a high adventure with the bikes on our way to the **Parque National de Ordesa.**

Have you, dear reader, ever sampled the thrill and wonder of a Pyrenean sunrise? If not, do so before the old legs turn the wheels more slowly and the rheumatic demons attack your joints. I crept out at 5.30 a.m. leaving my two younger friends in their sheets and blankets. In the icy chill of the dawn I zipped my jacket to the neck and blew on my hands. I could not see the sun but two high peaks were peeping out of the velvet and dark blue sky with a pale pink flush on them. Sitting on the bridge and watching the delicacy of it all, I saw pink change gradually to a fiery glow that spread down the rock-ribbed heights, until the snowy whiteness was dazzling in the sun glory of a new day. Watching until the sunrise was complete.

Such joys are simple ones but so dear and loved by the keen touring cyclist.

Not a single person was astir in the whole Balneario to share with me the beginning of the new day. My two young friends gave blanket-muffled grunts when I went indoors to waken them.

After breakfast and by 8 a.m. the bikes were loaded. We were ready for our mountain assault — our intention to follow a 'camino mulas' above the spa to Brazato. Then to travel over the mountains to the Rio Ara to reach the **Ordesa park-via Bujaruelo** and the Bridge of the Men of Navarre.

When I saw a workman from one of the hotels putting plants out on to a wall, I went to him, opened the map and in halting Spanish asked him: "How about it". His swarthy face clouded over with amazement as he looked at me and then the bike. As he pointed to the 'camino', I suspected that the whole of Balnearios would shortly be told of our exploits.

Already the temperature was soaring as we pushed the heavily- loaded bikes upwards and on looking back after climbing some 500 feet or more above the spa, I could see the interested group of spectators watching our progress.

The two youngsters soon doffed their shirts. I compromised by hanging mine outside my shorts and adjusting my sun-hat (I like to guard my balding head against sunburn). Deep down below now was the valley we had followed the previous evening, drenched in sun glory and in sensational beauty; the lake reflecting the bright colour splashes from the encircling peaks.

Our muscles were soon in action, lifting the bikes round rocky obstacles and negotiating stony stretches of the track. With some surprise we came to a branching track coming up from Balneario joining ours a little way ahead.

Then it all happened so quickly. One moment we were alone with the Pyrenees and the next we had company. Men dressed in dark green serge uniforms who appeared like the proverbial jack-in-the-boxes from a hidden bend in the track. They were Spanish frontier guards sporting ugly-looking rifles and guns. We must have been in their binocular sights from our very step on the track. Perhaps they had been sent to intercept us? I do not know.

My cheery 'Buenos Dias' (at least I tried to make it sound cheery) was received a little coldly. But then none of them spoke or understood English. I produced Michelin, pointing to the track on the map, performing a pantomime act with my arms to tell them we were going over the mountains with our bikes. Oh no! I could tell by their manner that we would definitely not be permitted to do so and they in turn pointed with their arms, indicating we should have to go back to the Balneario.

I stood my ground. The next step was a demand for our passports, which were critically examined. Dark Spanish faces peered at our own and compared them with the passport photographs (there was a little laugh when they looked at mine).

Leaning there on the crossbar and trying to make conversation, I could not help feeling a little sorry for them. To think that such a beautiful country should need lethal weapons to protect her frontiers. I compared their hot heavy uniforms with our lightweight cycling dress. Was not there a look of envy as they studied us and the glorious cycling freedom we enjoyed? I did not, however, like the look of those guns and arguing was out of the question. Not wishing for a hail of bullets around the bottom bracket had we dared to defy them, we retreated with grace down the joining track.

We had only descended a hundred feet or so when we came to a small hump-backed bridge. Just beyond was a weatherbeaten old wooden sign bearing the almost obliterated words 'Lago Brazato'. We had been wrongly directed from the Balneario and could now understand the agitation of the frontier guards. We had been unknowingly climbing to an illegal way into France.

With renewed zest we began to climb again, first up grassy slopes along which the bikes could be wheeled with ease.

Then the real work began in earnest as the 'camino mulas' reared up. There was a passage by stunted pines growing amidst rocks — a sharp tangy and resinous scent pleasant in the atmosphere.

On the way to Lago Brazato, in the Spanish Pyrenees.

Then the very wildness of it all began as we climbed up and up at steep angles. Soon the Balneario was cut off from our view and we were utterly alone in this high kingdom of the Pyrenees.

How these mountains move me; lordly kings rising in high triumph. I felt achievement and delight at getting to know them. The morning was wonderful, the sunshine and the Pyrenean glory was ours and high summer clouds were there, curling majestically above snow crested pinnacles.

Still upwards we toiled and wilder it became. Often our shoes and wheels dislodged rocks and stones, so we kept a respectable distance behind each other. There are those who say a cyclist wheeling his machine can get anywhere a mule can but, from now on, I shall raise my cycling hat to all mules who walk Spanish 'caminos'.

We crossed a small snowfield, and I made a large snowball to fit inside my sunhat to cool me down. How sweet and delicate were the minute flowers I stopped often to admire, growing from odd pockets of soil in rocky interstices.

The end was to come suddenly. Topping a rise we came to a plateau verged by a larger snowfield and there it was, the Lago de Brazato, blue and dazzling white in the rocky upland bowl of the mountains.

Mere superlatives of mine cannot do justice to the sight. Every peak was clearly defined against the sky, flanks burnished with the sun and below the lake of sensational beauty. Liberally floating on it were large 'icebergs' of snow many several feet thick. With absolute dismay we looked at our 'camino mulas' that skirted the mountain above the lake, which vanished into a large and extremely dangerous snowfield.

Above the snowfields were savage rocks and scree and the field sloped 45 degrees or more right into the lake. One false step with our loaded bikes would have been immediate disaster. An icy plunge into the lake could have possible fatal results. Over there beneath that ridge, where there was a prominent dip, was the elusive track. So near and yet so far away. Over there, we should have been enraptured by the splendour of the mighty Vignemale.

Once over there, also, it would have been all downhill, down, down and down, to distant Torla beyond the Ordesa Parque where we had hoped to stay the night. Instead it would take us almost a full day to get there from the Balnearios.

Just to see this lake had been worth the journey. My intention had been to have a swim in the lake to cool off but when I stepped into the shallows and dipped my hands into it, it was as if I had been stung by a thousand bees. Even my dark sun-tanned legs turned blue with cold, and my teeth chattered like the frontier guards 'machine guns'.

I soaped myself thoroughly and did manage a good splash and rub with the towel. How I glowed and sparkled after it was all over and how good was the mug of coffee that followed.

It was early evening when we reached the Balnearios again, and I could see the smiles on the faces of one or two of the people as if saying: "Told you so!"

The 'camino mulas' had beaten us. In recompense we had the miles and miles of glorious freewheel to look forward to on virtually-deserted roads. It had certainly been the hardest cycling day I had ever experienced and yet one of the most perfect.

I know that the Lago de Brazato in the pure harmony of its setting will always be a joyous vision to me. Who knows, perhaps I may not be able to resist the impelling urge to return before my cycling days are over, to challenge again the Pyrenees above Brazato.

12

"Like a Wet, Bedraggled Moth"

I HAVE always been enchanted by poetry, especially poetry of nature and the countryside. I often browse with the poems of Tennyson, Keats, Browning, Spenser, Shelley and a host of others who gave contributions to our literary heritage.

One evening I idly turned the pages to Wordsworth and read: "A slumber did my spirit seal", the first line of a poem of just two verses.

To me it was the master poet of **Lakeland** expressing the lovely sense of harmony and slumber but with the spirit waiting to be awakened. The more I thought of it, the more I was picturing Lakeland slumbering away in the hush of wintry days. So vivid was it all that the urge to capture this Lakeland atmosphere and mood could not be ignored.

Plans were forming. I knew I would just have to go searching the inspiration that had promoted Wordsworth to write and enshrine his thoughts in one single line.

I would go to **Hawkshead village**, where the young poet had spent his early schooldays. Then my way would be up, along, and over Hawkshead Hill to **Coniston**, where I should find the lake placid in the quietude of the morning. Then I should seek the high Tilberthwaite Fells and the secluded wooded ways to **Little Langdale**. The little tarn there would lead me on a thrilling rough way to the foot of the well known Wrynose Pass. The majesty of the Langdale Pikes would quickly come into view and in turn would lure me. I would come to Blea Tarn, so snugly embedded beneath their shadow and there, lulled by the soft murmur of the water and the wintry spell, I would sit. In the perfection of this Lakeland setting I would remember the words of Wordsworth that had brought me here and the magic of his memory and pen would be my contentment.

When I mentioned my plans to my good cycling friend Steve, he did not even raise the usual quizzical eyebrow — then he is used to my unusual cycle 'doings'. He accepts them without question, being content to 'tag along'. In any event he was equally keen for a wintry weekend in Lakeland.

Little did we know what was to be in store for us. Our Lakeland 'slumber' was to coincide with a period when Lakeland was to experience 48 hours of continuous rain, hail, and gale-force winds!

It all began in the cycle shed at **Hawkshead youth hostel**, where a fitful morning had brought the stinging cold rain. As we strapped on the saddlebags and donned leg spats, capes and caps, our spirits were definitely at a low ebb. The hostel lane to the Hawkshead road was awash. Without hesitation we turned our wheels towards the village; one never passes Hawkshead without a look around.

Ordinarily the village is choc-a-bloc with Wordsworth 'pilgrims' who come to browse around and look at the poet's grammar school; and to visit the church and stand before his schoolboy lodgings. On this early morning it was virtually deserted. Even in the rain it was good to seek out the many hidey-holes and secluded haunts that the village knows and which are almost unaltered since the poet's days.

A few turns of the pedals and we were at the junction of Hawkshead Hill and the Ambleside road. There we just had to leave the bikes again to walk the surrounds of the Old Courthouse which stands near the junction. This lovely old building with its quaint windows, archway, and mellowed old stones, has monastic links, and was used as a Courthouse by the monks of Furness Abbey.

The hill soon had us out of the saddle, the road streaming with water, with a steady drip, drip, drip of raindrops down our faces and noses as we pushed our way ahead. All was grey and gloom before us, yet there was to be a most welcome harbinger of the far-yet-distant spring to give me joy on this wintry morning and I just had to stop to savour it.

What I had seen in the dripping hedgerows were minute hazel catkins, barely a half-inch long. Pale green and hard, they made a brave display; forerunners of the dancing yellow 'lambs tails' that are such a spring delight.

On pointing them out to Steve, his only response was a whimsical grin and a non-committal grunt. Looking at little catkins is not his cup of tea. He then muttered something about the hot coffee and cakes he was looking forward to when we reached Coniston.

On top of Hawkshead Hill there is one of the finest memorial 'horse wells' I have even seen. There is a long trough for the horses and a seat for the horseman, who also has his own little basin, a most elaborate affair made in iron. The last time I had stopped before it, a hot sun was melting the tarmac. On that occasion, with a raging thirst, it had not yielded one drop of water. Today, with so much rain around, I did not want to drink.

Now the long drop to Coniston and its lake was before us. Warily we tested the brakes in readiness for the hilarious romp downwards. Thrilling was this freewheel, tyres spraying water to drench stockings and shoes, the rain stinging our faces. Any discomforts were ignored in the sheer exhilaration of it all.

This descent normally gives the finest panorama of Coniston Water with the dominant rising fells striding upwards to the frowning face of Coniston Old Man. Today, all was blotted out in angry swirling mist; dull grey shrouds were the order of the day.

Steve — all 14 stone plus of muscle and brawn — as always 'left me standing'. When at lake level with the road now hugging the shores, I was content to pedal slowly and leisurely, to appreciate the mood of the brawling and scolding water and to sample alone this display of nature's tempestuous spirit.

During the holdiay season Coniston caters well for its visitors. Many excellent cafes and snack bars are available, but on cold, wet, wintry days its a different story. How disappointing, for we had both so looked forward to 'elevenses' in Coniston. The village was deserted; most sensible people obviously being indoors hugging fires. Eventually we found some warmth and solace inside the church, which is a veritable treasure-house of Coniston's history. I even found a memorial to the lady who had 'bequeathed' the horse well on Hawkshead Hill. The church too remembers John Ruskin of literary fame and after reading much about him, I walked to the churchyard to look for his grave, surmounted by a beautiful carved cross, with many carvings depicting his works.

We had left the bikes in the shelter of a yew tree and when I later went to collect mine, Steve's was not there. A little uneasily I hastened to find him in the village, there to find him standing on the pavement, one hand holding his cape over his saddle and the other holding the remains of a large meat pie to which he was just applying the final demolition bite. The wily fellow had managed to find a butcher's shop open and his face

Grey shrouds on Coniston Lake and "like a wet, bedraggled moth", near Blea Tarn.

beamed with pleasure. "So much better than looking at Ruskin's grave", he said!

Saying goodbye to Coniston, we pedalled towards **Yewdale**, the beck of the same name skirting our road, racing down in spate. The beck would be with us for some time and the road would take us to the heart of the dale.

On fine days, Yewdale is a friendly little place, nurtured by the splashing beck and the rugged upstanding fells all around, make it a delightful picture. Today it was in stormy mood and the picture was not inviting at all although we were to have some consolation as we turned on to the minor road to **Tilberthwaite**, where I had promised to show Steve Tilberthwaite Gill. The waterfall there is a thrilling spectacle.

Lakeland has many 'gills', in secret and secluded places, each offering character and interest. For sheer majesty and wild water display, Tilberthwaite is without compare, although the initial approach is disappointing.

After securing the bikes we strode the rough rain soaked pathway, over the debris and litter of the many past years of quarrying in the area. Soon we were dipping down to the beck, thankful for the steep descending steps. When at beck level it was an awe- inspiring picture, leaping and prancing like a mad thing down to the valley. A footbridge took us to the far side until we reached the high footbridge that serves as the viewpoint for the waterfall itself. The narrow ravine echoed to the thunder and tumult and dense rising spray merged with the falling rain. The water below was being whipped to a creamy whiteness with deep pools boiling like some devilish brew. We did not linger long because of the spray drenching us thoroughly but to have seen this spectacle in such stormy conditions was ample recompense for the effort we had taken getting there.

Back to the bikes, then we pedalled the short distance to High Tilberthwaite. On passing through a farmyard and on opening a gate it was farewell to tarmac as we swung to a forest way that would lead us to **Little Langdale**. Steve was calling for food again, and within minutes we had found shelter, a disused quarry 'cave' where we would at least be dry for our meal. The morning newspaper was the tablecloth, two flat stones our chairs and with the sandwiches made we feasted royally appreciating the hot tea from the flasks, bringing warmth back to our bodies and bones.

On this rough woodland ride and walk, becks, young springs and freshets were everywhere. With a carefree abandon we splashed our way through. The background symphony was the noise of the wind in tree-tormented boughs. Once out of the woodland we hailed the spread of Little Langdale before us. The dale unfolds to Little Langdale Tarn nestling in the embrace of the high flanking fells. First of all there comes Slater Bridge, a pictorial gem of Lakeland, a slender arch which straddles in a most impressive manner, the beck flowing from the tarn. We could not pass it by — even though it meant climbing the step stile and squelching through the field to gain the pathway — for you have to see it at close quarters to admire its construction. What a picturesque survival from a bygone age it is.

A pathway above the tarn took us to a walled lane that dipped us down to tarmac, twisting and winding in the gloom and disappearing to the grey menacing clouds was the Wrynose Pass.

Our intention had been to wheel the bikes a short distance up the pass, then swing on to a track that would have taken us over Blea Moss and so follow the beck from Blea Tarn. Our soaking feet and our flagging spirit rebelled against the idea. Instead we decided to walk the steep ascending road to the head of Great Langdale, where near the summit we could walk down to the tarn.

There should have been tantalizing views of those well-known Pikes but they were well hidden in curtained clouds, although we were afforded one fleeting glimpse, before the gloom enclosed them again. The road streamed water, and the dark fells looked so inhospitable. We climbed slowly chatting to each other about the day, the ride and the evening warmth and shelter and good food that would eventually be ours when we arrived back at Hawkshead youth hostel.

We stopped just below the summit where a path would take us down to Blea Tarn. Leaving the bikes we began the last 'splodge' of the day to the waiting tarn below. From the many glorious contributions to Lakeland's heritage of beauty, the tarns stand out, so many of them in endless delight.

Such is Blea Tarn, with its dimpled shores, its trees of swelling glory and those magnificent fells rising to meet the overshadowing Pikes of the Langdales — the sort of scene where a poet could let his thoughts wander and his pen record words of beauty.

This then was the spot Wordsworth had lured me to on this wild wintry day. I stood there alone (Steve had wandered off somewhere) looking at it and thinking.

'A slumber did my spirit seal' had become a nightmare. Instead of placid dreamy waters, wind-whipped waves curved above the leaden-coloured surface and the rain lashed down in angry turmoil.

This was nature in relentless mood, thrashing at the tarn and the fells and sending the pounding rain squalls over the mountains. All feeling and sense of slumber had gone, my inward spirit had been roused. I was experiencing a wild and satifying exhilaration.

Steve had now reappeared to disturb my day-dream. He stood with a most amused grin on his wet streaming face, as if to console me. Perhaps Wordsworth at that very moment, in his Elysian domain, was looking down with pity and offering his commiseration to the two cyclists standing by Blea Tarn.

Holding the billowing capes down in the now gale force winds, we turned away and walked back towards the waiting bikes, like two wet, bedraggled moths.

13
The Cotswolds Ways

SEE the soft green willow springing
Where the waters gently pass
Every way her free arms flinging
O'er the moist and reedy grass

A SCORE or more time I had read the verse. Each and every time the word beauty had stolen a way into my heart. With half-closed eyes I would picture the scene — a gentle corner of age-old England. The urge to go and find the spot for myself could not be ignored.

The verse was one of many contained in a slender volume of poetry that had come my way in most unusual circumstances. Titled 'The Christian Year', it had been published 150 years ago. The book had been forwarded to me as a gift from a fellow countryside lover and the accompanying letter implored me to "visit the soft southern uplands of the Cotswolds" to see and revere it through the gifted pen of the author of 'The Christian Year', the Reverend John Keble. To this friend I shall always be grateful for having introduced me to the **Cotswolds** ways of Keble.

John Keble was born at Fairford, in 1792, and after a happy childhood he studied at Oxford, he was ordained in 1816, taking charge of 'twin parishes' and where I shall take my readers in due course. At this stage, however, please join my good cycling friend Eddie and I on the spring day we discovered 'Keble country', when cycling was sheer perfection. 'The Christian Year' was in the saddlebag, to be opened and read many times during the day.

Our 'Keble morning' had come bright and sparkling. Blue skies and high-trailing white clouds were overhead. The sun shone goldlike and warm as we busied ourselves with saddlebags, cooking stove and milk bottles in the small cycle shed at **Inglesham Youth Hostel**. It had been our first-ever visit to this small and homely hostel. 'Simple grade' in

The book of 'The Christian Year', together with a photograph of John Keble.

character, but definitely my type of hostel. So much better than the 'special' or 'superior' ratings.

A short distance up the road to Lechlade was the old track to Inglesham church — a veritable gem of the past. Though not a Keble church, it detained us for half-an-hour or so. Then it was the turning to Lechlade to the Cirencester road, and the few short miles to **Fairford** where our Keble story would unfold.

Now if you have always been a good cyclist and are not afraid to die, you will have no qualms about visiting Fairford church, but if you have been a bad one . . . Oh, Dear me! One look at the 'Devil Windows' in the church will send you quickly packing, and pedalling like fury to be away from it all.

There is nothing like these windows elsewhere; and they tell a full biblical story. There are angels and apostles, Eden and Hell, but what horror is portrayed in the 'Devils'. There are green devils prodding with red-hot pokers, a blue devil with webbed feet. There is a master devil — Satan with long tail and enormous teeth swallowing some luckless soul. Red hot fires are there all a'glowing, and some unfortunate beings are having their bones crushed in a mill!

After this nightmare of hell, it is a relief to admire the remainder of this gracious old church, especially its beautiful tower and rich carvings. We were seeing it framed through a lattice work of blossom-laden trees, and there was the morning play of sunshine and shadow over those soaring pinnacles. As pretty a picture one could wish for, so in keeping with the traditional Cotswold scene. Inside the church we saw our first memorial to John Keble: "Scholar, Poet, Parish Priest, Revered as a Leader of the Oxford Movement — born at Fairford 25 April, 1792, died 29 March 1866".

The Keble family have been well known for generations here at Fairford. Living in the house where John Keble was born was the Canon Edward Keble, descended from John's brother Thomas. Canon Keble had been the vicar of Fairford for many years but had retired. A letter to him previously had resulted in a ready invitation to visit Keble House and a ring at the bell brought him beaming with pleasure. As with the courtesy of his calling, we were made welcome and motioned inside.

How pleased I was when he produced for our inspection, the very first edition of 'The Christian Year' (the book went through 92 editions). It was thrilling to see many notes penned by the author in small, neat

Eddie chats to Canon Keble in the garden of Keble House, Fairford, where John Keble was born in 1792.

handwriting, hailing memories when the quill pen held sway. Other rare books, lovely old furniture in the study and photographs were shown. Over coffee and cakes, he nodded his approval at the 'Keble Way' we had chosen for our literary trail. Perhaps there was a little envy when we had talked enthusiastically about cycling?

Lovely indeed are the small rivers of the Cotswolds. Their names ring music as they roll off the tongue and course their respective ways — Windrush, Evenlode, Dikler, Churn, Coln and Leach. Each enjoys its own particular charm to tempt the tourist on his ways of discovery. It was the River Coln that was to attract our attention for a long spell, as we turned aside from Fairford to seek the lanes of Quenington. Immediately there was a beautiful view of Fairford church seen above the water meadows of Coln, with sheep and cows grazing in contentment.

John Keble knew these lanes well, often accompanying his father who was vicar at Coln St. Aldwyn. I like to think of him lingering by the river in the flower-strewn meadows:

> *Be your title what it may*
> *Sweet the lengthening April day.*

Also seeing the flush of leaf burst in the woodlands, the unfolding pageantry of nature in a countryside welcome:

> *Every leaf in every nook*
> *Every wave in every brook*
> *Chanting with a solemn voice*
> *Minds us of our better choice*
> *Needs no show of mountain hoary*
> *Winding shore or deepening glen*
> *Where the landscape in its glory*
> *Teaches truth to wandering men;*
> *Give true hearts but earth and sky*
> *And some flowers to bloom and die*
> *Homely scenes and simple views*
> *Lowly thoughts may best infuse.*

We found **Quenington** village drowsing in the noon silence of the spring day — and not a soul was around as we freewheeled down towards the church. Two magnificent Norman doorways have survived the centuries, reminding us of our historical heritage. Were you to turn the pages of the Domesday Book you would find the mention of a church here. I sat in the old oak pew by the door, the silence was uncanny and from the walls strange stony carved faces equally in silence looked down at me.

In front of the village green of Quenington is a small stone bus shelter with a seat. As there were no buses expected for some time we used it for lunch. A call at a nearby house produced water for the pan, the seat made an admirable table to spread the cape and tumble our victuals on. It was good to sit there looking down at the drowsing village. The signpost at the verge told us it was only three-quarters of a mile to **Coln St. Aldwyn,** the next village on our literary trail.

It seemed we had only given the pedals a few turns, and were gently coursing downhill, when I just simply had to stop to gaze at the rare scene of fragrance and quietude before me. The River Coln was fully revealed making a fitting foreground for the village of Coln St. Aldwyn nestling above the firm green prospects of the water meadows, and so inviting.

How well the river captured the mood of the afternoon, slipping below its attractive road bridge, and all a'shimmer with sunbeams. It made the daintiest of spring pictures, curving its sylvan setting where the well-fed cattle added pleasantry to the vista. Just beyond the road bridge was a pleasing little backwater, and I stopped to open a gate and walk the banks of the river where it gave a cool, green and glistening view of a garden nearby. Fat Mallard ducks waddled in front as I walked a path. A swan glided over the water in regal splendour and through the camera view-finder I could see Eddie on the road patiently awaiting my return.

Poor Eddie, he endures my many stops and delays with a sense of good humour. As we walked up the hill to the top of the village, he chaffed me about my exuberance. I told him I would be stopping again within minutes; the village church would claim my attention for some time.

Keble's father (also called John) was vicar here in 1782 and served the parish for many years, although he preferred to live at Fairford. I liked the memorial window in the church to both Johns — father and son. I liked, too, the manor-house and several houses that displayed the traditional Cotswold stone.

We bought supplies at the village shop. The good lady behind the counter was eager for a chat and showed interest in our cycle ride in Keble country. Then to **Hatherop** we turned by leafy lanes and quiet ways towards the twin parishes of **Eastleach Turville** and **Eastleach Martin**

In Hatherop there is a road junction, and as we approached there was that 'pinging-snap' noise that all experienced cyclists know immediately is a snapped brake cable. Eddie welcomed the stop as I delved in the tool kit for my spare inner-wire. He gave a satisfied sigh as he sat on a convenient seat nearby with hands clasped on lap in somnolence. The repair only took ten minutes or so; it was a real shame to waken him up but that elusive River Leach was not far away. The inspiring story of John Keble and the literary inheritance he gave to Christian England waited to be discovered.

Passing time will never dull from memory my first glimpse of the twin parishes of Eastleach Turville and Eastleach Martin, and I give thanks for seeing them in the afternoon hush of a perfect spring day. Down there was the kindliest of scenes — the River Leach rippling its way and dividing the two parishes, so that a church on each bank looked over to each other. There was a road bridge, but I had only eyes for the perfect specimen of clapper bridge, and from the end of it a stone path led a way through massed daffodils towards St. Martin's Church.

This was countryside England and its inherent beauty at its very best. I promised I would introduce John Keble's twin parishes. Here they were, in a captivating corner of the Cotswolds, remembering the poet priest who was to enshrine his writings in 'The Christian Year'.

He was minister here for eight years from 1816, and naturally passed over the clapper bridge hundreds of times; so much so that it is affectionately called 'Keble's Bridge'. What is more, there are willows fringing the river and I was beginning to experience the warm glow of inner satisfaction. At long last I was seeing the self-same view of them that prompted Keble to write his verse.

In addition to ministering to Eastleach, he had the curacy of Southrop, a village we would be seeing shortly and during his stay there 'The Christian Year' came into being. Into it he poured his innermost love of the soft Cotswolds countryside, weaving, as it were, a glorious tapestry of word-beauty in testimony and devotion to his religious faith and calling. Each poem with its appropriate religious message, links the varying moods of nature through the four seasons, with the timeless meaning of the festivals and holy days of the church.

After seeing what I consider to be the setting of my favourite verse of the willows, 'The Christian Year' was opened again at the last verse of the same poem and sitting on Keble's bridge I listened to the gentle cadence of the river below whilst reading it again and pausing to look around at the sheer perfection of this little secluded corner of the Cotswolds:

Where the thickest boughs are twining
Of the greenest darkest tree
There they plunge, the light declining-
All may hear, but none may see
Fearless of the passing hoof,
Hardly will they fleet aloof:
So they live in modest ways,
Trust entire, and ceaseless praise

Eddie had left me to my reverie and when I joined him after walking the path of the daffodils it was to visit both these gracious churches. Time was when the twin parishes had their respective Lord of the Manor, who built their own respective churches. Both of them cherish some 800 years of history.

Alas, poor St. Martin's has no heating, lighting or music, and is not used but nevertheless it is preserved so well by the village people. On the other hand, a stones-throw away across the river, St. Andrew's boasts these three essentials of church necessities and has a beautiful Norman doorway. How pleased I was to find a small glass covered case in the chancel, the book of 'The Christian Year' inside, opened at the appropriate page for the day. Old records tell of the many times John Keble, who was a fellow of Oxford, riding to the village on horseback and crossing the bridge that was to bear his name.

In 1966, on the centenary of his death, there was a commemoration service in both churches and a procession with a choir and orchestra. All of them passing down the 'daffodil path' and over Keble's Bridge.

Again Eddie was so patient, as I poked my way into all nooks and corners of the Eastleaches. Nay, I even climbed dusty belfry steps, brushing cobwebs away to look at the bells. They say the bells of St. Andrew's would ring: "We ring best", and the little church of St. Martin would reply: "We too, we too". It was to the present priest-in-charge that I was indebted for this story.

Time was passing so quickly in such idyllic surroundings. As I focused the camera for the last time, I could see Eddie, astride his crossbar, foot on pedal and waiting to be off. I joined him for the short remaining distance to **Southrop**, and the last Keble church of the day.

First of all, there was to be added spring raptures in the lane we cycled. Colonies of rooks were building in uppermost branches, their cries loud and raucous, yet this noise could not drown the jubilation of lark song overhead. Every hedgerow was prolific with primroses and there was bursting new life everywhere. The lane skirted the River Leach for a spell, and with pleasure we looked down to the river to see the willow pollards bending to the sun shimmered water and I appreciated even more Keble's poem of the willows that had brought me this way.

So it was through little Fyfield we rode to greet the Leach again and enter Southrop, where keeping the most massive of ancient barns company, we found the Norman church which was to reveal Keble memories again. As we entered I could not help smiling at the recollection of our meeting with Canon Keble during the morning, when unaccustomed to Cotswold brogue, I referred to the village of Southrop in the manner I thought it would be pronounced. Canon Keble with laughing eyes, had checked me saying: "No, it is 'Suth-er-up". For all that, there was a tranquil hush inside. We almost walked on tip-toe as if we were disturbing the thousand sleeping years the church has known.

On each side of the communion table were the stone effigies of a knight and his lady — Sir Thomas and Lady Conway dating from the mid-sixteenth century. On a wall I was to see an ancient memorial plaque to a Keble. This was to a "THOS KEBLA — Sen Gent deceased the 9th day of August Annodmi 1670 Elizabetha — VXOR POSVIT".

There was also another plaque to Edmund Keble Gent, departed this life Dec 30 - 1654. I was experiencing the satisfaction of knowing that from this lineage, I had spent an enjoyable half- hour with a descendant that very morning.

We were leaving the church when I glanced round a partition near the door, hanging there was a photograph of John Keble. From the photograph you could sense his shy and retiring manner, 'The Christian Year' does not even carry his name as the author. Eddie said: "We had better be off, if we're going to find somewhere to sleep tonight".

We welcomed the breeze that made our ride so enjoyable across the Cotswold pastoral scenery, to arrive eventually at **Oxford** at 9 p.m. and were fortunate to obtain the last two beds at the crowded youth hostel.

Oxford with its dreaming spires and beauty of sculptured stone was superb in the sunshine next morning. There could have been hours of sight-seeing had we wished,but it was the day we had to turn our wheels northwards. There was one place I just had to see before leaving, which for me would mark the finale of what had been the perfect literary pilgrimage of the previous day.

Keble College, Oxford.

After John Keble died in 1866, a fund was opened to establish a new college in Oxford. It was a fitting tribute to the poet, scholar and parish priest when Keble College was eventually built.

Too bad Eddie and I had chosen the wrong day, when the college was closed to visitors, but there was no objection when we walked beneath the entrance archway, to stand and look over the grassy lawn to the graceful lines of this respected seat of learning.

As I looked at Keble College the memories of the previous day were being kindled. The deep feelings he had enshrined into his 'Christian Year', especially my favourite verse of the willows had been the influence that had lured me to the loveliness of the soft Cotswolds countryside.

Moreover, my little verse of the willows had been lengthened by a companion verse, the scene of which I had also found. It had been, I am sure, in that lane of the primroses where the rooks had been building. Where Eddie and I had wheeled the bikes, Keble had also walked. It was the poet priest at his very best:

If, the quiet brooklet leaving,
Up the stony vale I wind
Haply half in fancy grieving
For the shades I leave behind
By the dusty wayside drear
Nightingales with joyous cheer
Sing, my sadness to reprove
Gladlier than in cultured grove.

14

Gatliff Hostelling in the Outer Hebrides

IT was so good to sit in the snug glow and warmth of the firelight with lazy flame patterns dancing on the age-old walls of the low humble room. The light from the oil lamp added to the atmosphere and from the comfort of the old-fashioned armchair, with a steaming mug of cocoa by my side, I was experiencing that lovely feeling of inner contentment that comes at the close of a perfect day of cycling packed with unforgettable memories.

Peering through the small window by the eaves of the thatched roof, dusk was slowly stealing the last of the day away. Beyond, over the grassy sward to the rocks and shingle of the shore, the sea sighed and heaved on the night tide.

These were magic moments and they were mine and mine alone. I would not have exchanged my lot for the proverbial 'king's ransom'. A lifelong ambition was being realized — staying and sleeping alone in a thatched Hebridean crofter's cottage. The cottage was on the small island of **Berneray North Uist** one of the exceedingly simple type of hostels made available by the Gatliff Trust.

Throughout the story of the Youth Hostels Association, there have been men who have left their names behind and their marks, to leave a rich inheritance of memories we today, and the youth of tomorrow can enjoy. Such a man was Herbert Gatliff, who despite his eminence and calling, was never happier than when blazing a trail of simple adventure in the Outer Hebrides. So fascinated did he become with the islands that the Gatliff Trust, which bears his name, decided to assist crofters in making available small crofts as hostels that otherwise might have been abandoned. The hostels are independent of the Y.H.A. but are open to Y.H.A members and members of other associations.

The rules are similar although there is no advance booking.

Essential facilities are provided. Those arriving should be self sufficient in their usage.

When I first learned of the Gatliff Hostels, the yearning for adventure was kindled again in my veteran years (but then I am still a youth at heart!) I knew I should not rest content until I too had travelled the 'Gatliff Trail'. With the bike I would wander the Hebridean scene. I would seek the sea and the shimmering sands, the panorama of hills and mountains and would look at the visible mysteries of our prehistoric ancestors, which are liberally scattered over the islands. Above all, I would relish in my travels the lingering bliss and joy of these simple hostels.

From my Lancashire home town, to Oban in the Highlands, is some 300 miles and although I do not often indulge in hard riding, I gave myself a complimentary pat-on-the-back when these miles had passed beneath my wheels in a little over three days. My hopes for sleep on the MacBrayne ferry before departure to South Uist was thwarted when I was told that first the Mull ferry would have to arrive and depart and that the Uist ferry would be equally some two hours late.

I had reserved accommodation for the night at **Lochboisdale**, taking into account the normal ferry arrival time of 11.30 p.m. So it was with some apprehension as to what my reception would be as I turned the pedals for my first time ever on strange and darkened lonely roads from the ferry landing pier at 1.30 a.m.

I need not have worried, for Mrs. MacLeod (God bless her), obviously used to the shortcomings of certain ferry sailings, was awaiting my arrival. Nay, there was a light shining like a beacon from her house porch to guide me there. She greeted me warmly with that charm and courtesy well-known in the islands and in a jiffy there was a welcome meal on the table, then sink into slumber in the most comfortable of beds.

Lovely it is to wake up in new surroundings on a cycle tour, but more so on an island. The morning had come dull and grey, I eagerly peered through the window over my ample breakfast and was pleased with what I saw.

The road from Lochboisdale soon links at a 'T' junction with the main narrow road that cleaves a northwards way above Atlantic shores. There are exciting causeways on and off the island of **Benbecula**, separating the Atlantic from the Sea of the Hebrides. Then there is a spectacular circular sweep around North Uist before the road terminates at Lochmaddy, the terminal for the mainferry to Lewis.

I find it so hard to resist place names on a map, for usually there are hidden surprises in store linked with events from the past. When I was at the 'T' junction there was a captivating lane before me, reference to the map indicated it would lead to a 'Pictish Wheel House'. I naturally could not resist its invitation and so it was I turned my wheels towards what was to become my first baptism, as it were, into the age-old story of Uist.

It was a lane to gladden my heart, bordered here and there with yellow iris and kingcups. Tarmac merged to pebbles and sand. My tyres were crunching sea shells as I nosed my way towards the coast. Not a soul was about and the cool green glistening machair was profuse with sea pinks providing the most pleasing of contrasts.

I found the Kilpheder Wheel House with ease — a Pictish dwelling dating from the 2nd century — which originally boasted a turf roof. I stood in the centre where the hearth had been and let my mind wander down the centuries to the days of its occupation. The shifting and wind-blown sand of the passing years had covered most of it but as I stood there I could appreciate its design — shaped and fashioned by ancient skilful builders.

How satisfying it was to stand there listening to the sound of the nearby sea, the screaming of gulls, and the noisy wind that was to high-tail me the length of South Uist. On my way back to the island road I passed several thatched cottages and sniffed appreciatively at the scent of burning peat.

The morning mist was lifting. Grey was giving place to white and blue. The mountains were coming out of hiding, revealing themselves in friendly screens. The Hebridean scene was being revealed to me in perfection, the little dainty houses, the several crofts of thatch, the lochs and lochans. The elusive lanes were calling again and at a place called **Vaccisary** I turned to the coast because I wanted to approach **Howmore** by the back way. Besides I had promised myself lunch at Howmore, where I should come to the first of the Gatliff Hostels.

Down these lanes were sea sounds, the tangle scent of seaweed fresh island greens and flower carpets of joy. I revelled in the ecstacy and pleasure of cycling at its very best. In this happy frame of mind I came to Howmore to see the little thatched crofts dotted here and there blending beautifully to a pattern of life that remains unchanged.

The door on which I knocked was the house of the warden owner. After exchanging the courtesies of the day, she pointed out the hostel. "Just up the hill — the one with the blue door". I liked the snug, homely quality about it. The trim roof of thatch, the white sturdy walls and the blue door. Everything was spic-and-span inside, in-keeping with the spirit of those who use the hostels. There was a tap to fill my pan, a stove to cook my food and a table to spread my meal and I sat there the most contented of men.

From the window I looked down to a medieval chapel and monastery. Naturally this had to be explored. Here were gaunt ruins reflecting a religious age of fervour all tumbled in confusion, yet symbolic in sanctity and meaning. This lovely spot had been destroyed at the Reformation. I looked at chapels dedicated to St. Mary, St. Columba and the MacDonalds, where a carved stone displayed the family crest.

I had to resist the urge to stay at Howmore for the night but there was so much more of the island waiting. So many surprises, so many inspiring scenes. The South Uist mountains were now revealed as a lovely shimmering garland and they too, seemingly beckoned.

But it was to the northern road I turned my wheels again, beneath sunny summer skies, the wind on my tail and the pedals just being turned lazily in the pleasance of the afternoon. I reached **Loch Bee** and the road causeway over it. What I at first thought were seagulls on the water proved to be swans sunning themselves in white splendour, constrasting beauty with blue.

Then it was to the causeway over the Atlantic by South Ford and on to the island of Benbecula and shortly afterwards another look at the Atlantic at North Ford, as I passed off the island and came to North Uist. Here I had the choice of ways. I could have chosen the longer circular sweep round the northern coastline to **Lochmaddy** but instead I took the shorter way there, as the food bag needed replenishing.

In stopping to greet an apple-rosy cheeked woman who was chivvying a cow away from her cottage garden, I enquired where I could camp for the night. With a flourish so typical of Hebridean hospitality, she opened the gate and invited me to "Camp anywhere here, sir!" I chose a flat sheltered spot, overlooking a small loch and my meal was prepared in the summer glory of the evening.

The gulls dipped gracefully over the water, the sound of sheep and cows came from the hillside, the rushes and bents by the lock shore stirred in the breeze and in this happy atmosphere my first day in the Hebrides was ending. Tomorrow I should be lured on my way to fresh haunts of loveliness, as I took up again the Gatliff Trail.

After my usual hefty breakfast and with camp chores out of the way, I loaded the bike for the last few miles of my stay on Uist. It was to be a rare morning of coastal display when I should see the mosaic of little creeks and sea channels, blending sands with colour and smell the scented fragrance of the machair.

I had ample time at my disposal to enjoy it all as well, before I should arrive at the tip of North Uist, where I should say farewell from the small passenger ferry that would take me to the **Isle of Berneray.**

Up in these high places of the island lilting Gaelic rules supreme. Often I had a good laugh as I opened the map to see the veritable jumble of place names that defied pronunciation. I would not have had it otherwise, for this lovely ancient language is in keeping with the heritage of the past.

How I was enjoying this tour, just content to be lazily pedalling along, stopping frequently just to browse and stare and pointing the camera with scant regard for the inflationary cost of film.

'Newtonferry' said the small sign, as a minor road came into view. This was it — the last few miles and I was having it all to myself, save for the sheep and grazing cows. Just as my early introduction to South Uist had been halted by a 'Pictish Wheel House', so was my impending farewell to be delayed by a 'Pictish Broch', a ruined structure I could see on a small island in a loch. Its name was 'Dun an Sticir', and I was pleased I should not have to get my feet wet, for there was a stone causeway over the loch to the island. What a chequered story it hoarded, dating to the second century. At one period of its tempestuous history it had been besieged in 1602. I liked the way all the ancient monuments I found had a most informative potted history on a board for the benefit of visitors.

I poked my way into inner tunnels, and walked the grassy surrounds of the massive walls. History is never dead, it is there to be preserved by such visible remains and the stories they echo and retain should never be allowed to die. Here again were swans on the loch, gulls mewing overhead, the play of cloud shadows on the hills and the sea, all reflecting the beauty of the morning.

Only a handful of scattered dwellings marked Newtonferry and I was a little puzzled, until I saw the sign 'Newton Jetty' and the secondary road leading to it. I rounded a small bay almost level with golden sands to see cows walking in file formation the wrinkled tide to tempting pastures on a small headland. A little distance on I just had to stop again to gaze in rapture at one of the finest seascapes I had ever seen.

The sun was lighting the bay in dancing colours ranging from vivid blue through turquoise and varying shades of green and merging to the white and gold sands of the shore. The sands gave way to the lush short grass, flower strewn as if delicately embroidered. The fat clean sheep grazing there completed to perfection the picture.

It was a fitting farewell. Topping a small hill I coasted down towards the Sound of Berneray there to find the jetty and wait for the ferry.

I took out the small stove that fits snugly into a side pocket of the saddlebag. The water bottle was emptied of its pint and over coffee, biscuits and cakes, I rejoiced at what Uist had given to me. Waiting out there on Berneray Island was the second objective on my Gatliff Trail — a little thatched croft.

I watched the ferry butting its way through the swell and was greeted by the ferryman from the island who told me there would be some delay, as a 'cargo' had to be loaded and shipped to Berneray.

A lorry eventually arrived at the jetty and from it jumped three sturdy men of Berneray, who in a twinkling began transferring building material from it to the boat. I watched spellbound as bags of cement were tossed around and stacked as if they were mere bags of sugar, to be followed by other supplies. They laughed and spoke in Gaelic and still laughing they lifted my bike aboard and wedged it firmly with the assortment of supplies beneath the wheelhouse. It only needed one hand of a Berneray giant to lift it.

I later discovered that a distant relative of this man had been 'Giant Mackaskill of Berneray' — born 1825, height seven feet nine inches, weight 500 lbs. He emigrated to Canada and eventually died there.

What a lively crossing it was to be, sparkling with laughter and good humour. A pat on the back for my veteran years, a hearty handshake and being regaled with a rousing Gaelic song especially for my benefit. I was even 'toasted' with a generous tot of traditional Scottish 'golden water' and I warmed inwardly to it all. So good to feel this display of Hebridean friendship and to be accepted by these men of Berneray.

I waved goodbye as I topped the slope leading from the small island jetty to reach the island road swinging me round the sickle curve of the bay. What joys, what delights were mine as I sampled the peace and tranquility there, so that I still catch my breath in wonder when I recall it all. Here were jumbles of lobster pots, coloured sea floats, ropes and boats. Small crofts dotted the slopes of the bay, many of thatch and lovely white walls. The sea shimmered beneath the afternoon sky of blue and white clouds and out there were other little islands and the mainland of Uist I had left behind. What I was seeing and experiencing now would be cherished cycling memories of the future.

I had not far to go, for when the tarmac finished I pedalled a pebbled path towards a gate and a large house. On wheeling the bike through the field entrance behind, there was a lovely spread of sward, bordered by a huddle of thatched crofts, small and appealing. It was the very essence of the **Berneray** scene — a picture of haunting quality. My immediate feeling was that a welcome was there and the croft nearest the shore with the neat new thatch was the hostel.

What a friendly little place it was to be. Neat and tidy and having the simple comforts so dear to the walking or cycling wayfarer. Later when washed and refreshed I took on the role of 'chef de cuisine' so that I sat down to gammon steaks, new potatoes and vegetables with fruit and custard and cheese and biscuits to follow. All rounded off with two mugs of coffee.

Word of my coming had been noted and I had a call from Miss MacKillop the warden. She looked the picture of health and beaming a

Berneray Gatliff Hostel.

Miss MacKillop, Warden, of Berneray Gatliff Hostel.

welcome, she enquired: "Was I all right and was there anything I needed?" I thanked her warmly, appreciating such lovely hospitality.

I have already told of my evening at Berneray hostel, so now I shall ask my reader to join me next morning on the island jetty as I boarded the boat that would take me to **Leverburgh in Harris,** where I should take up again the Gatliff Trail to new adventures.

On the ferry (which first calls back at Newtonferry) was a cycling French family, also bound for Harris. I listened with interest (as well as trying out my own limited French) to their experiences and impressions of their tour.

Leverburgh had a first class shop to stock up the foodbag and from here I disdained the main road to **Tarbert,** preferring the way by the eastern shore. By so doing, I was able to visit **Rodel** almost at the toe of Harris, where the venerable monastery church there is one of the most treasured wonders of the Hebrides.

A far different scene was now being presented as I followed this shore road. I was seeing for the first time mighty cliffs being pounded by breakers seething and boiling white. High above them I could hear the roar. Inland too, was a grim spectacle of nature's supremacy — a landscape of great ribs of exposed rocks sweeping in savage contours and formations to the South Harris mountains. Without doubt, this is the most savage of the Hebridean landscape, and yet there is the stimulation and appeal of the myriad of sea and land lochs as atonement for those wild mountain approaches.

I could quite easily have made a detour to stay the night at Stockinish youth hostel a very popular one of the Scottish Y.H.A. chain but instead

I linked up eventually with the main road to Tarbert to complete my arrival in the little seafaring village by a long thrilling freewheel.

Tarbert is the terminal for the ferry to Uig in Skye, and also for Lochmaddy in Uist, but for me, now, there was the sharp angled turn to the secondary road towards **Scalpay Island**. I was now experiencing a feeling of inner excitement, preparing myself for what was to become one of the finest adventures of my cycling life. As the road crossed the narrow neck of the sea exit loch of Laxadale, there was no mistaking the footpath swinging away from the sharp road bend, and climbing steadily to wild solitude.

It was the beginning of the footpath way to **Rhenigidale**, where I should find the most dramatically situated of the Gatliff Hostels. As I wheeled my heavily laden bike along it, little did I know what was to be in store, before reaching the hostel.

At first it was easy going, and I romped along in fine style, wheeling the bike steadily upwards and although a few misty dark clouds were frowning on the tops, was not worried. Backward glances revealed spectacular seascapes, even in the now grey light and I stopped at the summit cairn to prepare for the eventual descent towards the sea for the final push and walk to Rhenigidale.

At this stage, dear reader, if you should be thinking of following my wheels to Rhenigidale, please do not do so. By all means wheel your bike to the summit cairn, but leave it there. From this point take only the bare essentials for the rest of the way, for the pathway from the cairn is extremely dangerous with a bike and perhaps an unwary slip or tumble could result in a fall from which recovery would be impossible. The ending would almost certainly be instant death.

Though the route to Rhenigidale I had received from the Gatliff Trust had warned me about the path, I had foolishly ignored it and on proceeding from the summit cairn, I stared unbelievingly at what was before me. The path descended alarmingly in savage zig-zags from 900 feet to the heaving waters of the loch below. My scalp tingled with fear as I began the nightmare descent. Inch by inch I slowly progressed, stopping at every hairpin turn and twist, as I repeated to myself "Never again, at least with the bike!"

With my heart in its rightful place again, I could have sang a doxology as I wheeled the bike along. Despite the now dull evening this Rhenigidale pathway was pure joy. In its wild solitude it dipped and climbed and hugged green hillsides by the sea. I reached Rhenigidale to be greeted by almost the whole 'township' of ten who stared incredulously at a cyclist wheeling his bike in their midst. The hostel was pointed out to me as "The building with the red roof." I entered to find five enthusiasts there to welcome me.

There was that simple but homely feeling about the hostel and I liked what I saw. Surprisingly there was an 'upstairs' for the men and by the time I had prepared my bed for the night, there was a shout from below that "supper was ready". To my surprise, an extra place had been prepared at the table. I joined in the communal savoury meal that had been prepared by the ladies and how good it all was.

When chores were over there was that sense of friendship and fellowship that is the very basis of satisfied happiness. It is one of the riches of life, enjoyed and retained by those who seek the lovely atmosphere of these simple-type hostels.

It was to rain heavily throughout the night and morning came with Rhenigidale shrouded in dense mist with a light drizzle falling and visibility down to yards. Over breakfast I had been mulling over the problem of how I was going to negotiate the 'hill of the zig-zags'. I had decided rather than risk disaster, I would make three climbs, first with the bags and the last with the bike. Even so, conditions would be treacherous especially after the heavy rain.

Into this Gatliff 'saga' there now step two tough but charming cycling girls — Caroline Palmer and Sarah Wood, medical students from London. To reach the hostel they had sensibly left their cycles behind at Laxadale, putting up a tent for their equipment. Leaving at the same time as me, they took one look at my loaded bike and insisted on my unloading the panniers, handlebar bag and saddlebag, saying they would carry them up the zig-zags for me. Leaving me with just the bike. With grateful thanks I accepted their kind offer.

I should think Rhenigidale is one of the remotest spots in Britain enjoying the title of 'township'. Out of the population of 10, there is one child, a schoolgirl, who had her own schoolteacher. Supplies come by sea although the postman walks the hill of zig-zags three times each week. During my walk to the hostel I had met a venerable old man of 79, who told me stories of his seafaring days in many parts of the world.

By the time I had re-arranged the bike, Caroline and Sarah had been swallowed up in the mist. Feeling much happier with my lighter load I gave a silent "cheerio" to Rhenigidale, wheeling the bike along the pathway again that had given me so much joy the evening before.

Despite the forbidding conditions and subdued light, there was an enticing spell around as I walked the wet grassy way. I could hear the calling of unseen gulls, the rush of spate-filled burns, the roar of waterfalls, and the sign of the hidden sea below. Then it was I was descending to **Loch Trollamarig,** and beyond and up there was the waiting 'hill of the zig-zags'.

Passing time shall never dim from memory my ascent of the hill on a morning when nature was in relentless mood. Perhaps in my aged years, I shall look back on it as a nightmare. I was thankful for the stout shoes I was wearing, which gripped the wet and treacherous surface so well. Pausing often for breath, I progressed upwards, foot by foot, taking the utmost care on each one of the zig-zags. 'Inner Man' was telling me off too! "Here you are Albert, perched on this Hebridean hill at a mature age when you should be in your armchair with your slippers on and patting your grandchildren affectionately on the head. Why on earth do you do it?" "Rubbish", I replied. "What does it matter as long as I feel young in heart and with the spirit of adventure coursing through my veins".

Slowly, oh so slowly, I pushed, wheeled, coaxed and cajoled the bike upwards. Never was a summit cairn more eagerly welcomed, when I last stood by its side, with the rest of the way to **Laxadale** now easy going. I caught the two girls up and helped them to 'strike' camp and load their cycles and together we rode the few miles back to Tarbert. The feeling of tarmac was by now so strange below the wheels.

At my invitation and over fish-and-chips and a steaming teapot, we recovered and talked about the morning's adventures. Afterward as we said "cheerio" to go our respective ways I thanked them again for their kindness. It was now raining heavily as I pedalled towards new adventures and delights.

Herbert Gatliff died in 1977 in his 80th year and to my profound regret I never met him. He had a distinguished career and was a senior officer in the Treasury and also with the Ministry of Town and Country Planning. His undying interest was in the Hebrides which he loved so dearly and the founding of these simple crofters hostels to whet the appetite of adventurous youth (not forgetting the adventure loving 'veterans'). Lovely it would have been to have met him at any one of these hostels, now his memorials. Rank and calling would have had no significance. We should have both been endowed with the friendship of the hills and the mountains and the great outdoors of nature's heritage. In the happy atmosphere we would have yarned the night away and my farewell would have been a hearty handshake of thanks accompanied by a sincere: "Well done, Sir".

POSTSCRIPT:

Since the above chapter was written, the Gatliff Trust have opened another hostel at Claddach Baleshare North Uist. Rhenigidale has now got a road. This will no doubt be welcomed by the little 'township' it will mean easier access and more visitors. One hopes that the appeal and magic of this remote spot will not be marred in any way.

15
The Old Familiar Ways

W INSTANLEY. . . Water" — the loud shouted command came from the kitchen, to echo down the old stone flagged passage where I was helping with a washing-up chore in the most ancient of shallow stone sinks there. "Coming", I shouted back and my washing-up companions doubled up with laughter as I hastily filled a two-quart ladle-can with cold water then almost ran with it to the kitchen. There I lifted the great iron lid of the steaming fire boiler to empty the cold water inside.

The voice had been that of Mr. Lewis, the hostel warden, as usual with his spectacles pushed up to his forehead. With a chastising face, yet beaming with merriment and in the bluff manner we knew so well, he looked me in the eye saying: "Tha knows th'rule lad", as indeed I did. A two quart ladle can of hot water taken out of the boiler by the gleaming brass tap at the bottom had to be replaced immediately by a ladle of cold water poured in from the top.

Oh but this was the most lovely of old kitchen ranges, shining with 'black-lead' and maintained with loving care. The companion to the boiler on the opposite side of the burning coals was the oven. And now from out of the seemingly cavernous depths, Mrs. Lewis in a crisp neat apron and wearing a starched bonnet on her head, was taking lovely fruit pies, cakes and 'oven bottom' scones and buns. My tastebuds were tingling as I watched her liberally dusting the appetising array with caster sugar. I lingered in the mouth-watering and lovely aroma of the fresh baking whilst chatting to them both.

Then there was another loud shout, this time from the passage — "Hey, what about this washing-up?" Mr. Lewis laughingly pointed his pipe in that direction and said: "Tha'ad best bi gooin!"

This little scene took place around 1936. The place was **Slaidburn Youth Hostel.** I was in my tender teenage years and the delights of the magic world of cycle touring was being revealed to me. How well I remember it all, together with a hundred other Slaidburn memories as well. Fifty years on I once again sign the hostel house book and peep inside that kitchen on yet another visit.

The old stone in the cobbled courtyard of Slaidburn Hostel, was used during 'coaching days,' to place new tyres on the coach wheels.

Yes, these autumn, veteran cycling years of mine are still as exciting as the first ones. I remain, as ever, young in heart, so dedicated to leisurely touring; charged with thankfulness and contentment that our lovely English countryside is still there for me to enjoy.

Today I came up to Slaidburn by one of the old familiar ways. The lanes were quiet. The homely quality of the Bowland landscape, the rolling fields, meadows and fells and the little farms and cottages have, as always pleased my eye. One of the 'perks' of the retired cycling pensioner is being able to choose his day for yet another cycling adventure — when the weather is just right — and he knows that many good things will await him.

From my Lancashire home town it did not take me long to thread a way through the pockets of industry. At Longridge beyond Preston, I stopped to make a few purchases for the saddlebag. It had been good to coast down to the very threshold of Bowland, where the lanes unfold pleasant vistas with every mile.

I always like the steep curving lines of Longridge Fell, serving as a backcloth, yet as a fitting introduction to the Bowland scene. I had him in the picture for quite a spell until the lanes took me away from him towards the many becks and small rivers that feed the Hodder. Without doubt, a jewel in the Bowland crown.

I had already seen the lusty River Loud coursing through its meadow and I now found myself eagerly awaiting the short dash down to Doeford Bridge, where not only should I see the Hodder for the first time of the afternoon but also the confluence with it of the Loud.

I stopped on the bridge, for leaning over bridges to look at rivers below is a pastime that begins in boyhood and is still as enjoyable when one is

Slaidburn Church.

a dad or grandad! Some heavy rain earlier in the week had provided a most exciting display and I looked at the spate flooding river, brawling and scolding and pounding at the sturdy buttresses of the two curving arches of the bridge. I climbed a step-stile to walk the soaked banks to see it all to advantage and to watch the eddying currents of the Loud at the 'meetings' just below the bridge.

From the saddlebag, I took out one of the cream buns I had bought in Longridge and opened the flask to enjoy the snack with the Hodder for company. In the days of yore I should never have dreamed of eating and drinking tea at Doeford Bridge, for at the top of the short hill beyond was Apple Pie Cottage — a mecca in those days for all wheelmen coming this way. There, in the homely atmosphere of a garden shed, dear Mrs. Blezard from the nearby cottage knew the way to a cyclist's heart, to cater for his hungry needs.

Massive pint mugs from which you could drink deep were the order of the day; while she would be continually replenishing the table with great apple pies and other goodies. Laughingly, she would divide them into sensible 90 degree portions which you had to eat with both hands. Ah, the perfection of home-baked pastry, the memories of juice soaked chins and the sounds of mmmmmm. It should be no surprise that 'Apple Pie Cottage' was our affectionate name for it.

The old cottage and the garden shed as we knew it are now gone; they are a nostalgic memory of the old familiar ways. Alas, 'Apple Pie Cottages' and cyclists 'pint mugs' of tea are a rarity now.

I would now be saying "Cheerio", to the Hodder for a spell, for it would be hidden from view until I would approach it again nearer Whitewell village. What a lovely river it is. How well it nurtures the Bowland scene, matching beauty for beauty with each mile of its flow. There is the wild romp down from the fells of its birth, the serene and fragrant flow through its rich valley and the final touch of splendour when the eventual joining with the River Ribble at Mitton takes place.

With the familiar ways to Whitewell now before me, I was revelling in the lazy meander, letting my mind wander down the years and recalling the little adventures, the events and happenings that had been mine in this Bowland domain. There was so much to enliven the scene; the sunshine gilding the Bowland panorama and dancing cloud shadows patterned on the fells. Soon the mature tree line ahead would display the steep descending banks to the Hodder.

Minutes after, there it was, roaring in spate filled fury, making a thrilling picture through the boughs and branches of the shrouding trees.

In contrast with the steep descending banks and on the far side of the lane, are some high shattered rocks; and perhaps the passing cyclist might feel his scalp tingle as he reads the notice "Beware of falling rocks". You can either change into a higher gear and pedal in fury past the spot, or "trust to providence".

So prominent and waiting now above the Hodder was the Whitewell Hotel, famous since the 16th century, offering five miles of salmon and trout fishing on the river. It has always been a well known Travellers' Inn, with 'elegant' accommodation and high class catering. Looking at it today again, brought back a memory of the thirties when we could be served here with a large teapot for fourpence each, and we could eat our own food. Times have changed. Yet the cyclist calling there can be assured of excellent fare, with the atmosphere of the traditional coaching inn to be enjoyed.

Whitewell, too, has its little church, linked in many ways with the history of Bowland. Fascinating stories come down from the misty beginnings of time when ancient man lived in the dark caves on the far banks of the Hodder. Scientific excavation has revealed many finds about his occupation there. The Romans knew the valley well and were around for some 300 years. But it is the links with the ancient 'Forest of Bowland'

An old 'Bowland' signpost, preserved in a garden at Bashall Eaves.

over which the spell of the centuries lingers. Large herds of deer roamed the valley and there were offical 'Keepers' and 'Officers' who maintained strict Forest Laws in the age of the Bow and Arrow. In the days when we pedalled the familiar ways every signpost was topped by a small carved effigy of the 'Man of Bowland' with his tightly stretched 'bow' and 'arrow' at the ready. I know where is still one preserved in a garden and I often look at it with affection as I pass by.

Behind the Whitewell Hotel the river is in full view and a pathway over a wall halts at a viewpoint to give one of the most distinctive and satisfying views throughout Bowland. The river comes down in a gentle curve from the embracing fells above, hiding the thrilling defile of the

The Horseman's Signpost, Dunsop Bridge.

'Trough of Bowland'. Even the most casual of passing cyclists cannot fail to be deeply moved at the beauty presented there.

I always like Burholme Bridge that quickly follows Whitewell, a hump-backed structure of old vintage, in keeping with the rural pattern of Bowland. Up to a few years ago, it was the 'marker' for the boundary between Lancashire and the West Riding, with the Hodder serving as the dividing line.

Beyond the bridge, adding to the scares of the 'Falling Rocks' before Whitewell, there is another scalp-tingling notice that the road is "liable to subsidence and flooding". I then recall a black wintry night when the floods caught me unawares, when suddenly my feet and pedals were under water!

I have already mentioned the old signposts of Bowland. At the junction marking the turning to Dunsop Bridge there is a veritable gem of a signpost recalling the stagecoach era. It is the 'horseman's signpost' and consists of slender arms springing from a worn carved stone pillar. The arms are at eye-level, so that they could be read by a horseman as well as the stagecoach driver. The stone pillar bears the date 1739 as well as the chiselled distance to Slaidburn, Clitheroe, Hornby and Lancaster. A modern signpost now overshadows it but I like the way the distances carved in stone differ to the modern successor.

"3 miles to Slaidburn" said the 'horseman's signpost' and "4 miles" said the modern sign.

To spend the last few miles on these ways would be deeply refreshing, with a score of memories tumbling in my mind and with Bowland and its river providing poetry and character, even though the afternoon was fading.

Limestone had come into the scene, attractive snaking walls interspersed with hawthorn; and over them were the inviting and snatched glimpses of the river embosomed in its valley. To me, the Hodder on these approaching lanes to Newton village is one to challenge the famous River Wye view from Symond's Yat. Equally inspiring, equally majestic in the harmony of green.

I always regard Newton-in-Bowland as the "village of wells", for there are several taps and pipes pouring water and these, with the warm grouping of cottages, and the radiating narrow lanes to the fells, make the place a happy one. In those old cycling years, there used to be a little 'shop-cum-cabin' where we used to enjoy tea and snacks, and where always a motley collection of cyclists would gather.

Dusk shadows were preparing to steal the afternoon light away as I walked the steep hill out of the village, with but one mile remaining to Slaidburn. In those halcyon days of youth and exuberance, I would most certainly have romped up this hill in a mad caprice, challenging my companions to be the first to the top. Now, after exhausting my lowest gear, I am content to walk and take my time over it.

At the summit, a mantle of grey was taking over the sky and the dusk shadows were stealing their way into the folds of the fells. I switched on the dynamo for the last short descent, the twist and turn and then the last flat run into Slaidburn. So good to see the waiting village again, so lovely the age-old church that seemingly bids a welcome and keeps a fatherly watch above the village. A few more turns of the pedals and I was at the coach yard entrance to the hostel removing the saddlebag.

If I may, dear reader — especially my younger ones — I will regale you and take you back down the years to the 'thirties and what it was like to arrive in Slaidburn then, after coming to it by the old familiar ways.

The hours we then worked were much longer so that by the time we had arrived in the village our lamps would have been lighted. 'Lamp lighting time' was always a ritual, for though there was still a sprinkling of oil lamps around, acetylene or carbide lamps were vogue. After weeks of saving, I had acquired an acetylene generator (affectionately called a 'chip-shop'. The generator was mounted on the top tube with a rubber pipe snaking to the lamp on the fork boss. How lovely was that lamp with its opening door of magnifying glass, a ventilating hood on top, and a tiny green glass window in one side, and a red one in the other. How well I maintained it, and how often I burnished and polished it.

There would be at least six to ten of us on a hostel weekend, and at the appropriate time of approaching darkness, the cry would echo "Lighting up time, lads!" There was the 'turning on of the water' on the acetylene lamp, the sniffing to see if the gas was coming through the burner, and then the 'plop' as the match ignited it — then the careful adjustment of the flame.

With our assorted beams flooding the road, we would arrive at a Slaidburn of mellow lights spilling from cottage windows onto cobbled surrounds. Electricity did not come to the village until after the war years and I look back with nostalgia at the remembrances of these oil-lamp lit cottages, on our short ride up Church Street entering the hostel courtyard, wheeling the bikes over the cobbles and then extinguishing the lamps with the smell of carbide lingering in the shed.

The hostel was a former coaching inn and, happily, much of the atmosphere is still there. In the bike shed is a niche that formerly housed the lantern and in the old stone building we would take off our saddle-bags, just as we do now, and enter by the back door.

Our shoes would echo down that stone flagged passage I mentioned with the stone sink and the water pump on which always sat the 'two-quart ladle-can'. There was no hot water in the hostel but we could always take a ladle can of hot water from the fire boiler — as long as we put one back — "Tha knows th'rule lad!"

Oil lamps were everywhere, sending mellow beams into each room and flickering shadows to the ceiling beams. My word, how carefully tended were those lamps. Tall chimney glasses sparkling and the brass work all aglow. Woe betide any hostellers who dared to touch one or to turn the light up or down; Mr. Lewis would quickly be there. Each lamp was a revered joy to him; he knew each one and its personal idiosyncrasy.

He was always there waiting in what had once been the bar of the coaching inn, spectacles pushed up to his forehead, carefully checking each hostel card as we signed the housebook, paid our 'one shilling' overnight fee (5p). Those days of the early thirties were hard ones, our pockets were always 'light'. More often than not, we could not afford the one shilling for a hostel supper. 'Self cooking' was on oil stoves, later primus stoves were provided.

No matter what we ate, there was always the ritual of Mrs. Lewis cutting those fruit pies, cakes, and 'oven bottom' buns and scones. As at 'Apple Pie Cottage', they were divided into four pieces and each piece cost threepence!

Evening chores over, we would sit in the firelight glow in the Common room, chatting with other men and girls who had cycled or walked to the hostel. Mr. and Mrs. Lewis would join us and we would yarn the night away. Tired after our long working week but relishing the magic of these precious weekend hours, we would climb the stone steps to the outside dormitory, eager as always for the delights of the morrow.

Tonight I stand in that cobbled courtyard, my saddlebag under my arm and experience contentment and thankfulness that continued good health still enables me to look forward to and enjoy hostel weekends awheel, even after fifty years. With appreciation I look at the preserved large circular 'wheelstone' by the door, often mistaken for a grindstone; but it was used those long years ago to fit new tyres to the large coachwheels, the hole in the centre accommodating the hub.

I can picture strong-armed men placing the hot iron tyres over the wheels; can imagine the smell of sizzling wood as water is poured. I can sense the impatient stamping of horses on the cobbles, the creak of harness and leather and the welcoming voice of the innkeeper.

Within the hostel there is a merry chatter of voices and laughter, a cycling club from Bradford is there, as well as a few schoolboys — two of them hostelling for the very first time. There are brightly coloured cycling jerseys, track suits and jeans, a far cry from our plus-fours and riding breeches of yesterday! Good fellowship prevails and I am happy to join in with it all. After all, I am still young in heart and always there is that happy bond of friendship when cyclists are around.

I enjoy a most appetising supper — succulent sausages, roast potatoes and vegetables, sponge pie and custard.

The two cycling schoolboys are still full of wonder at this new cycling world of hostelling adventure. Perhaps a little enviously, I look back and recall my own self-same experience at their age.

I have the chore of washing-up in the kitchen and I look to where that ancient black-leaded range once stood. The range of the boiler with its brass tap and the matching oven and the burning coals. There is piping hot water at the turn of the tap and I can sense Mr. Lewis looking over my shoulder with "Tha knows th'rule, lad".

Back in the Common Room, a coal fire is burning brightly and the chairs are grouped around. The 'Hark to Bounty' Inn across the way has claimed some of the Bradford boys. The two schoolboys I have been chatting with have gone to bed and I sit alone by the comfort of the fireside. I am in meditative mood as my dreams of the years are turning in my memory.

"I have been coming here", I say to myself, "for over 50 years by the old familiar ways and yet my love and appreciation for the bicycle and the lifetime of magic and happiness for my chosen way to spend my leisure hours has not been dimmed in any way". I am meeting the young and the future followers of cycling and hostelling and I know full well that they will love and appreciate the beautiful countryside that is ours, especially here in Bowland. Perhaps later, they too will be able to follow the old familiar ways as I have so often done.

Who knows, someone who will be as old as I am now, may recall this chapter and will casually say in the hostel common room : "Do you know what, a chap called Winstanley used to come here."

16

The Lure of the Larig Ghru

WHENEVER and wherever touring cyclists gather, and the talk drifts round to favourite haunts of Britain, the Scottish Highlands are bound to be mentioned.

The talk will be of mountains, of lochs and glens and then someone will surely mention the **Larig Ghru**. Should that someone be a cyclist with adventurer's blood coursing through his veins, there will be a deep sigh for the memory of this king of all the Scottish passes.

It conjures up a vision of rugged and dominant summits frowning down on the pass, as it cleaves its way through a tough and untamed region, merging its sensations with its unforgettable excitements.

Many times in my fledgling years I had listened to the tales of the 'old-timers' who had 'done' the Larig. Always it had been an ambition to go there myself, to see this wonderful Scottish scene. Strange that the opportunity to realise my ambition did not come until I too was in the autumn years of my cycling life.

Here I was, with my good cycling friend Steve, camping at **Bynack Lodge** on a morning following a day of pure perfection in Glen Tilt, eager and as excited as the proverbial schoolboy, knowing that this was the day of the Larig. What a dull and listless morning it was, with all the mountain tops wearing grey nightshirts and with drizzle in the air.

The gloomy atmosphere accentuated the spooky feeling at being at the ruined lodge, once a proud mountain home, now a shattered ruin. Yet Steve hummed a merry tune as he sizzled the eggs and bacon and I simmered the porridge. I must tell you also that it was not yet 6.30 a.m. (did I hear someone say: "must be nuts").

By eight we were away, fording the boisterous Bynack Burn, where on the far side we reached a rough drove road that soon tumbled us down to **White Bridge**, which is the link with the popular track coming up from Braemar to the Linn of Dee. This is the accepted way to the Larig by cyclists who have stayed ovenight at **Inveray Youth Hostel**.

It was the first time I had seen the royal river of Dee and I immediately warmed to it. In the quiet of the morning it was good to follow the track hugging the river, dipping and winding our way and steadily climbing. We were both pleased that as yet, there had been no difficulties or encumbrances.

Unhappily, the sunshine we had hoped for was not coming and the morning began to deteriorate. We looked at the might of the Cairngorms waiting to challenge us, the track soon to take us to the great defile cupped beneath their flanks. How I enjoy this freedom. Of being at peace with the mountains, to experience their broody silence, as if they are listening or watching your every mood. Here in the Glen of the Dee approaching the Larig the Cairngorms are at their very best. So wild and majestic, with Ben Macdui at 4,296 feet the big 'daddy' of them all.

On the far side of the Dee were Ben Vrottan and Cairn Toul, big brothers of 'Mac' with the lofty extreme of Cairn Toul menacing the pass with the Devil's Point. I did not think the 'Devil' was taking a liking to us, for his snout was cocked above the track in a black and sinister manner. To further deride us, he was causing the clouds and mist to descend, cloaking the mountain profiles in a seemingly grey world of mystery.

As we drew level with the 'Devil', there was a depressing picture of the deep and gloomy Glen Geusachan, which is embosomed between the Devil and Ben Vrottan, with its burn hurrying to join the sister river in Glen Dee.

Worse was to follow, for the mist gave way to rain and Steve in his carefree manner remarked we were due for a spell of Scottish "liquid sunshine". We donned the capes but they were to hinder us, as the track became rougher, with boulders and rocks to be negotiated. Quite soon we were soaked.

Most of us have heard of 'bothies' — small wooden or stone structures tucked away in odd and solitary places in Scotland. Well the Larig has one of the very best, the **Corrour bothy** important enough to be pin-pointed both by the Ordnance and Bartholomew maps.

We espied it from some distance, a precious jewel as it were, set some distance above the river and a welcome sight in the rain-soaked glen. God bless the men of old who had the foresight to build these havens of refuge, so appreciated by the hill and mountain wayfarer. Every success to the men (and women) of the Mountain Bothies Association, who are

120

doing such sterling work in renovating many bothies that have fallen into disuse and disrepair.

We squelched and splashed a muddy way through oozing peat and bog to reach the bridge over the Dee leading to the bothy and opened the door to a snug and dry interior.

Off came the wet jackets and capes. In a twinkling the stove was roaring away. Oh the absolute ecstasy of those first sips of scalding coffee. Thick wedges of bread were cut for man-size sandwiches and hefty slices of cake for 'afters', followed by two more cups of coffee.

Meanwhile I looked around at strong and sturdy walls, candles in rough sconces, flat boulder stones worn smooth with long contact with corduroyed-seats of men who had used them down the years. I would not have exchanged it at this moment for any plush lounge in any four-star hotel.

Outside, the rain lashed the window, the mountains still wore night-shirts. We could barely see the elusive Larig trackway on the far side of the river for the mist. I knew there would be some reluctance to venture out for some time, but if need be, as countless of others have done, we were well equipped to spend the night there.

Atonement was to come from the 'Devil down the Glen'. Steve remarked: "It's getting lighter outside". So it was. He made the roof of the Corrour Bothy wring with a wild Sassenach yell of "Hoots mon" as he hastily danced around, packing his bag, rolling up his cape so eager to be on his way. I was performing likewise.

The misty grey was lifting, mountains became shadowy patterns as the storm abated. The clouds diffused to silver and then the sun struggled through.

There was a definite spring in our step as we regained the track, turning our faces and wheels to the steeper contours ahead. With a fresh sweet breeze on our faces and high-flung mountain glory all around us. Up and up we tramped taking the rocky track in our stride. Exercising the utmost care with the bikes as we coaxed and lifted them over rocks and boulders.

The peak now claiming our attention on the far side of the glen was Braeriach at 4,248 feet lording it above the others. His upper flanks gleamed black shining and silvery after the rains and he had many high pockets too of the unmelted snows of the past winter.

Our many backward glances revealed the Dee in all its haunting loveliness and above all, there was the delightful play of light and shade from the clouds now scudding the summer skies.

We were then halted in our tracks. At first stared unbelievingly at what was before us. My first view of the famous Boulder Field of the Larig Ghru was quite a shock and I just had to stand and stare to take it all in; realising also that this was the final challenge to the summit of the pass. It resembled a dramatic landscape of 'hell'. Boulders and rocks were scattered in profusion, blocking the whole of the upper confines.

Happily the way was well served with cairns, even so, both Steve and I were thankful we had stout stainless steel mudguards on the bikes to withstand the several bumps and bangs to which they were being subjected. Steve seemed to run out of expletives, all 14 stone of him, as he carefully tested each boulder before choosing his steps.

How many who negotiate this famous boulder field realise that a veritable geological wonder is beneath it all, for in nether regions, the infant Dee still flows. When the first section of the 'field' has been passed, you see and marvel at the first of the Pools of Dee that captures the thrilling spell of the Larig and the river, that is trapped in this lair of the mountains.

We safely crossed the lower boulder fields, passing the smaller pools and then began the long downward trek towards distant **Aviemore**.

Sunshine and scattered showers were to be our lot on the descent, a descent spiced with variety as more and more glorious prospects were opening up. Time was passing all too quickly, so that as we approached the tree-line and the first scattered pines of the beginning of the Rothie-murchus Forest came into view, a check told us that we had been on our way for some ten hours.

The evening was to come with a haunting loveliness, as the path entered woodlands and the sun cast golden patterns, lighting the glades and flushing every bough and branch in dazzling splendour. Unknow-ingly, we had strayed from the correct path and were surprised to emerge onto a newly made road with the Army in command.

They were as surprised as us. Good-humoured banter and a chat brought a ready invitation to follow the road, with a warning that we could expect a locked gate at the end of it.

Even this confrontation with the Army had its amusing climax. Suddenly there were loud piercing screams and yells as we were pelted with 'grenades' of pine cones. From a hidden trench at the forest verge jumped several young soldiers enjoying their joke and we joined in the good fun.

Free-wheeling down the road, within minutes we were negotiating the locked gate, which gave entrance to the highway by the shores of

At the start of the Larig Ghru, at White Bridge, and the rocky terrain of the Larig Ghru.

123

Loch Morlich. The loch looked so placid in the evening glow and it was so strange to feel a smooth surface beneath our wheels as we rode the length of the loch to the homely youth hostel there. The hostel was 'busting at the seams' but the good warden (bless him) said he had "never turned a cyclist away yet".

Lashings of hot water, a good scrub and a welcome change into dry clothes followed, then a giant meal put us in fine fettle.

I was experiencing a lovely satisfied feeling. A new chapter had been added to the memories of my cycling life. It was the memory of the superb crossing of the Larig Ghru. Steve and I indulged in our usual after-supper stroll to shake down the meal. A big full moon was riding the summer night sky; it silvered the far Cairngorm tops across the loch into gracious beings and the several snow pockets below their summits gleamed white in enhancing beauty.

There was a feeling of peace about the scene and the spell of it all to me, as I thought about the events of the day and these mountains that had taken a firm place in my heart. They had so enticingly unfolded for me and displayed in many moods the pass which in future I should regard as the finest in Scotland.

17

'Sentimental Journey'
to North Yorkshire

THE little old lady was most perplexed and didn't know what to do, or think of it all. Here she was in the village church, and before her, couched on the lectern of all places, was a mouse. It looked so perky and mischievous if you please.

There was no-one around, so in her thin nervous voice, she said: "Shoo". The mouse, to her surprise, did not move. The little old lady then plucked up courage, touched it warily with the toe of her shoe, but still the mouse did move. Her face then beamed in a smile, as she realised the mouse was made of wood and had been cunningly carved into the lectern.

The village church was at **Kilburn** in North Yorkshire, and what she had seen was the famous 'Kilburn Mouse', the work of master carver and craftsman, Robert Thompson. Thompson was born and bred in this beautiful village and he adopted the symbol of the mouse as his 'trade mark'. "Industry in small places", was how he so aptly put it.

How I love this delightful story of the old lady and the Kilburn Mouse, just as I love this delectable touring area of the **North Yorkshire National Park**. Here I was in the village again after an absence of some 30 years, recalling and reviving

Kilburn Church, "The church of many 'mouses'".

memories I had always cherished.

Malton in the Vale of Pickering had been the start of it all on a sparkling spring morning. As I pedalled the lanes towards the Howardian Hills, nature was bursting all over. There was that rich feeling of the freshness of the season, and that touch of countryside loveliness that makes turning the pedals sheer pleasure. Bright sunshine was overhead, the meadow flowers in patterns of colour, and the trees in budding and unfolding greens. For the first time of the year, I had peeled off my jacket and strapped it to the saddlebag, thoroughly happy with it all.

I like these Howardian Hills, well wooded and gentle. They were to be a fitting aperitif for the higher Hambleton Hills, towards which my wheels would be turned later in the day. I coasted down to **Coneysthorpe**, the village of the stately Castle Howard mansion and cast an appreciative eye at a sun-gilded stream dimpled with banks of primroses. The nearby crossroads, too, gave a striking picture of Castle Howard with the spreading lake before it. Though tempted to stop, my way was ahead and onward to **Terrington, Dalby**, and **Gilling**.

Morning coffee was now in mind but I waited until reaching **Ampleforth**, where the village inn offered first class service and a chat with the landlord. We were joined by a workman from Ampleforth College and I became an interested listener.

Gosh, it was warm work, pushing the bike up the steep hill from Ampleforth. I could not resist the invitation of an open gate near the top, giving entrance to a lush green field with a shady tree close at hand. It suggested a spot for a mid-morning idyll and I did just that. Spreading the cape, lying on my back, hands clasped behind my head and at peace with the world. A skylark overhead burst with melody, the warm spring breeze fanned my cheeks and I was thoroughly content. After all, to spend idle moments in meditation on a perfect spring day, is one of the unbounded joys of this cycling life of ours.

The spring day was getting better and better. Each turn of the pedals brought exciting vistas into view. I passed through little **Wass village** and then, in dramatic outline, seen in sun shadow, was Byland Abbey. Naturally, I would have to stop, but waited until I was facing the main entrance, where all was revealed.

The Cistercians who came here chose their spot well for their building of the abbey, where the lush and swelling meadows were sheltered by the hills. What we see today is a testimony to their architectural skill and devotion — still strikingly beautiful in its ruined decay.

I was now approaching **Coxwold**, and when there I decided to walk through the village, wheeling the bike — besides I knew full well there would be so much to see. If you, too, would seek a village of haunting

Shandy Hill, Coxwold, once the home of Laurence Sterne.

quality, where the past lingers on in a calm serene manner, do see Coxwold and search and delve into its fascinating past.

Here are trim small cottages, displaying pantiled roofs,which peep coyly at each other from either side of the street. There is an ancient almshouse, a village inn with a link with the past squire of the great hall ('The Fauconberg Arms') and the church standing high, enhances the scene so well.

Ah, but there is something else in Coxwold — a long low rambling house, with quaint and odd corners and higgledy-piggledy gables. Here there once lived a jolly old vicar,whose name was Laurence Sterne. His home became 'Shandy Hall'. He wore a long flowing wig, a velvet coat, shoes with great brass buckles and silken stockings, and always he radiated good humour.

I can picture him so well in 1760, when he was vicar of Coxwold Church, enjoying his good life in the village — especially as his gifted pen would bring him fame. From it came 'Tristam Shandy' peopled with the most extraordinary characters.

Shandy Hall has now become a literary shrine to Laurence Sterne lovers from all over the world but unhappily I had arrived on the wrong day to add to the number of visitors. Nevertheless, I was enjoying the scene, seeing that snaking great chimney breast, topped with its neighbouring red bricked chimney, several degrees out of true and making the most unusual of neighbours. I peeped through the gate where Sterne had his "hundred hens and chickens" and over the door I read the inscribed stone telling me that the good incumbent of Coxwold had lived here when writing 'Tristam Shandy' and the 'Sentimental Journey'.

Now the 'Sentimental Journey' followed 'Tristam Shandy' and received equal acclaim. As I read this inscription, my own mind was a'wandering down the years. Suddenly I was recalling a chapter from my own cycling life. I realised that since leaving Malton early that morning, I had been following the self-same lanes I had followed on that day 30 years ago as a family cycling man. My tandem had been equipped with a 'junior pedalling attachment' at the rear and my healthy and exuberant young daughter had kept up a ceaseless chatter of everything she had been seeing, whilst my wife, riding her own machine, beamed her approval of it all.

Now in these veteran years of mine, I can smile my contentment at the 'golden days' I have known.

I pedalled onwards to Kilburn village, happy at the recollection of this, my own 'Sentimental Journey', so awakened unknowingly by

A family outing 30 years ago. Our daughter was transported in a specially-constructed tandem attachment.

Laurence Sterne of Coxwold. I smiled to myself when I thought that my "exuberant cycling daughter" of that day has made me a cycling grandad, with equally healthy and exuberant grandchildren. I should like to think that, perhaps one day, they too may follow the wheeling ways I have loved so dear on an equally 'Sentimental Journey'.

I arrived in Kilburn village, to find it drowsing in the noonday quiet. I had caught it at its best, for usually it is teeming with visitors who come to see the 'Kilburn Mouse'. What a special and fascinating story it all is — this unique trademark of Robert Thompson, who was destined to become known the world over for his craft. He was born in 1876 and kept alive the ancient art and workmanship of the adze, specialising in church furniture with, of couse, the mouse on every piece.

How I laughed when entering the church, to find the vicar, who was just leaving — being stopped by a small girl, who asked him so innocently: "Please can you tell me where the mouse is?" The vicar, in good humour, said laughingly: "Just look around, and you will see 'mouses' everywhere". I offered my hand to the little girl and together we entered the church, just exactly as I had entered with my own daughter those long years before.

Her eyes widened and sparkled with surprise and amazement as I pointed out the 'mouses'. They were everywhere: on the pulpit, on the pews, at floor and eye level. There was even the one on the lectern.

On that day of the Kilburn church visit 30 years before, the tandem had been parked outside the Thompson workshop and was being critically examined by the workmen, who showed interest in the 'junior pedalling attachment'.

My daughter had told them all about it. "Although Daddy did all the work!" Judge my surprise when at the time we were presented with a carved ashtray, complete with its Kilburn mouse. Though a non-smoker, I still treasure it. So did my daughter for the rest of the tour. Each night it was stroked and fondled and tucked into bed with her.

Just as the Kilburn Mouse is small, the Kilburn White Horse is immense. I had seen him from many vantage points after having passed Byland Abbey. He stands proudly on the slopes of Roulston Scar above the village — a veritable giant of a horse 314 feet long and 228 feet high. It was the Kilburn village schoolmaster, who in 1857, began it all, carving the great animal on the hillside. Of course, he has no claim to antiquity like the other 'White Horses' of England, although for shape and size I think he is the best of them all. Unhappily, he does not stand on chalk, so he has to have frequent coats of whitewash, by willing volunteers.

There is a 'White Horse Walk', and a flight of steps leads upwards by his hindquarters, turning onto a pathway by his tail and flanks and along his back — then down his head, front legs, fetlocks and hooves, and so back to the starting point Visitors are discouraged from standing on the actual horse itself.

Having walked the 'White Horse' without the bike, so I was now to walk the White Horse Hill by Roulston Scar with the bike, taking my time on the several severe twists and turns, whilst climbing all the time, until eventually I met the busy Thirsk highway. I tolerated the main road for only a short spell, welcoming the respite of the side-turning to **Scawton village,** that would sweep me down to the waiting delights of Ryedale.

There is perhaps not another county in England so bountifully-endowed with monastic remains as Yorkshire. Each retains its own particular place and keeps its chapters in the colourful story of monastic England. Deep in Ryedale is one of the fairest of them all — **Rievaulx**, occupying a commanding situation and embracing the raptures of religious architecture. The Cistercians founded it in the 12th century, dedicating it to the Holy Virgin. During its hey-dey, it was perhaps the most prosperous of the monastic houses, enjoying rich agricultural lands and large flocks of sheep. Today, excellent restoration has been accomplished by the Ministry of Works, so that the ruins are seen to advantage from the well kept lawns.

I enjoyed seeing Rievaulx again in the pleasance of this spring afternoon, the sun touching the ruins in warming glow. On that distant day, too, the three of us had also enjoyed this abbey scene, lingering in the dale, until it was time to climb the steep hill out of the dale. This afternoon I had promised myself another Rievaulx treat — to walk the Rievaulx Terrace, so that I could look down on the abbey encompassed in the dale below.

From the days of the rich landowners and the elegance of the great gardens of England, comes the story of the creation of the Rievaulx Terrace. Over 800 men were employed on cutting a great terrace from the hillside above the abbey around 1758, and to enhance its beauty. A 'classical' temple was built at each end. First, I walked a marked pathway through woodlands. This in turn took me to the massive green level lawns of the Terrace and I walked to its end to see the 'Tuscan Temple'.

Owing to the now unsafe floor, the Temple was closed but I admired its Doric pillars, the ornamented upper frieze and, through a window, a strategically- placed mirror reflected the ceiling with the painting of a winged angel.

The second Temple — 'the Ionic Temple', complete with symbolic soaring pillars. To my delight it was open, and I stepped inside a 'Banqueting Room' to gaze upwards at the wonderful painted ceiling. This ceiling with its theme of Greek mythology and legend was completed in 1761, it having taken the painter four years to perform the massive task — the painting having been done lying on his back.

Goodness me, I had changed a film at the Tuscan Temple, and a glance at the camera counter told me I had pressed the shutter 20 times. As I walked back to the bike, I laughingly told myself — "Albert, my lad, curb your enthusiasm, colour films are too expensive these days!"

The way to **Helmsley** was now before me, but before deciding to seek accommodation for the night and with the precious hours of this spring day not be wasted, I opened the map for guidance — for something special that would put the finishing touch to my 'Sentimental Journey'. There it was but a mile or so away. The name was **Kirkdale**. As I pedalled the highway, I found myself eagerly waiting to see again the simple scene so fair I had long remembered from 30 years before.

The name Kirkdale is self-explanatory — but Kirkdale is in fact far more than that. For this 'Kirk' is a 'Minster', dedicated to St. Gregory, and it houses a time treasure unique in the whole world.

There was no-one around as I cycled the narrow lane towards the churchyard gate. I noticed again the venerable old yew tree seemingly keeping a sentinel-like watch at the beginning of the church path. In the tranquil atmosphere of this late spring afternoon, the silence was deafening and St. Gregory's stood in absolute solitude in the "Tom Thumb" dale. I opened the door of the porch and there, above, was the Saxon sundial. The sundial dates back to AD 1055, and is the most complete one in existence. Every letter cut into it is perfect and the explanation is that the sundial was covered by a layer of plaster until 1771 — hence its preservation.

The time-honoured charm of the centuries lingers on inside St. Gregory's. Such treasured old churches are veritable jewels of England with 1300 years of history all around you.

By no means was St. Gregory's Minster the only thing to see in Kirkdale; I coasted down to a small ford and a dimpling stream, where I left the bike to walk down a very much overgrown quarry, where in a limestone cliff-face I climbed and scrambled to peer into the openings of a cave.

In 1821 this cave yielded to scientific excavation hundreds of animal bones. When pieced together they revealed a story of amazing scenes enacted there. The bones were those of lions, bears, elephants, rhinoceros and other animals that had roamed the dale in our early history and yet they were too large to have entered the cave.

The explanation was that this cave was once occupied by hyenas, who had killed and dragged their prey to the cave. As I peered inside, resisting the temptation to indulge in a muddy crawl, my scalp tingled as I thought of all that had taken place there. If any man had been around then, he would have found Kirkdale most inhospitable.

As always when I am in such interesting surroundings and when there is so much to see, I lose all track of time. On checking my watch, I realised I should have to hurry to reach **Helmsley**, to see if there would be a bed to spare at the popular youth hostel there. Fortunately, there was and of the capacity of 40 staying there, 36 of them were cyclists. Does not that warm the cockles of your heart?

The cycle shed was bursting at the seams. A club of healthy teenagers, after a day's tour, seemed to be 'licking their wounds'. Gears were being adjusted, new brake blocks fitted, inner tubes were being repaired; there was chain trouble and two lads were busy with a spoke key on a banana-shaped wheel.

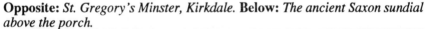

Opposite: *St. Gregory's Minster, Kirkdale.* **Below:** *The ancient Saxon sundial above the porch.*

I was in my element watching them, listening to their healthy and carefree chatter and appreciating their enthusiasm. My obvious advanced years was ignored in comparison to their youth and was secretly pleased when I was addressed as "Sir" asking my advice and assistance over the troubled buckled wheel.

Laughing and joking together, we coaxed it back into 'rideability', then altogether made a huge pot of tea to celebrate and chat over. They outlined their ambitious plans for the morrow; was not this the very essence and friendship of cycle touring?

Later, seated in a comfortable chair, a nightcap mug by my side, I had time to reflect on the events of what had been a superb spring day. The cycling lads were still in high spirits and chattering noisily.

Not only had my own 'Sentimental Journey' recaptured for a spell, precious memories I treasure of a period of my own cycling life, but it had sent me to look at the lair of wild animals, old churches and abbeys with their own enduring memories. There had been the White Horse and the 'mouses' of Kilburn. Best of all, there had been the jolly old vicar of Coxwold complete with his wig, velvet coat, silken hose and brass buckled shoes. His own 'Sentimental Journey' that had flowed from his gifted pen, would always be a favourite with me :

I am happy as a prince at Coxwold, and I wish you could see in how princely a manner I live . . . tis a land of plenty. I sit down alone to venison, fish and wild fowl, or a couple of fowls or ducks with curds and strawberries and cream, and all the plenty which a rich valley under the Hambleton Hills can produce. With a clean cloth on my table and a bottle of wine on my right hand, and I drink your health. I have a hundred hens and chickens about my yard, and not a parishioner catches a hare or rabbit or a trout, be it as an offering to me. I am in high spirits; care never enters this cottage . . . "